Exciting Ideas
for Ward Activities

PARTIES WITH A PURPOSE

Exciting Ideas for Ward Activities

BY
TRINA BOICE

spring creek
BOOK COMPANY
Provo, Utah

ISBN 978-1-932898-83-5
e. 1

Published by:
Spring Creek Book Company
P.O. Box 50355
Provo, Utah 84605-0355

www.springcreekbooks.com

Cover design © Spring Creek Book Company

Printed in the United States of America
10 9 8 7 6 5 4 3 2 1
Printed on acid-free paper

Library of Congress Cataloging-in-Publication Data

Boice, Trina, 1963-
  Exciting ideas for ward activities : parties with a purpose / by Trina Boice.
    p. cm.
  Includes index.
  ISBN 978-1-932898-83-5 (pbk. : alk. paper)
  1. Christian life--Mormon authors. 2. Parties--Religious aspects--Christianity. I. Title.

BX8656.B65 2007
254'.6--dc22
                                2007027428

"I am thankful for the
mess to clean after a party
because it means I have been
surrounded by friends."

———————————

NANCIE J. CARMODY

TABLE OF CONTENTS

CHAPTER 1

Your Sacred Calling

"Life may not be the party we hoped for,
but while we're here we should dance."

AUTHOR UNKNOWN

Congratulations on your calling! You're now the official Party King or Queen of your ward! You might be wondering how on earth throwing parties could be a spiritual calling. It is! How could even having ward parties be important in these perilous times we live in? They are! The events that you plan for your brothers and sisters are extremely important to their spiritual development. The time they spend together is sacred time because the Lord has promised that "where two or three are gathered in my name, there I am in the midst of them." (Matthew 18:20)

YOU will be providing that incredible opportunity for them! The goal for every program and auxiliary in the Church is to "Come unto Christ."

In the book of Acts we read about Paul, the apostle, and his effective service to the early saints. In chapter 13 we see an interesting statement about when he was serving in Antioch with some other members of the church there. In verse 2 it says, "As they ministered to the Lord, and fasted, the Holy Ghost said…"

A few lessons jump out at me in only a few words. First, Paul understood that while serving the saints he was really ministering to the Lord! Matthew 25:40 confirms the same truth: "Inasmuch as ye have done it unto one of the least of these my brethren, ye have done it unto me." Every streamer you hang, balloon you blow up or dish you wash for a ward activity is an act of worship and glorifies the Father. It's your testimony to Him. It's your offering of sacrifice and love. It's how you are called to feed His sheep right now. This is how **you** can minister to the Lord today.

Another lesson I see is when you combine service with fasting, the result is the Holy Ghost will speak to you! As you and your committee members plan activities for your ward, pray about the members and thoughtfully consider their needs. You have a stewardship over them now and have the right to receive revelation about how you can best serve them and help them become the saints the Lord knows they can become. He directs this calling in the Church. He knows your efforts will bless others and that hearts will be touched through activities you plan.

Your parties have great purpose! You will be providing an opportunity for members and their nonmember friends to gain a testimony of the gospel and to practice living its principles. You're not just serving dinner, but serving to build the Kingdom of our God. **It doesn't matter how many activities you have, but how many souls are reached.** Jacob and Joseph just might have been talking about ward activities when they said, "Wherefore we labored diligently among our people, that we might persuade them to come unto Christ, and partake of the goodness of God..." (Jacob 1:7)

Which kind of activities should be provided for the ward: spiritual or fun? How about both?! If the gospel of Jesus Christ is called the "Plan of Happiness" then we should be the happiest people around! Ward activities should be opportunities for members to feel the joy of living the gospel! We need to laugh and be united together.

Ward members want to have fun, but they're also too busy in their lives to just pass time with no deeper purpose. Even after playing a game or working on a craft project, a short spiritual lesson could be given to point out the gospel application in our lives. Make sure your activities meet their needs, whether they be spiritual, physical, emotional, intellectual or social. Provide activities that offer opportunities to develop talents, support and strengthen families, nurture testimonies and build self-esteem. When ward members see that you are planning valuable activities that enrich their lives you will have their support.

As you plan the activities, remember to ask:

+ How will this activity make us more Christ-like?
+ How can it strengthen our testimony of the Savior and His Church?
+ How can we increase community relations with this activity?
+ What gospel principal can we teach?
+ How can we support the auxiliaries of the Church at this event?
+ What ways can we delegate some of the tasks to get others involved?

It's helpful to have ward members fill out some kind of interest and talent survey to direct your energies towards activities that appeal to them, as well as provide opportunities for them to shine in front of each other and for their hearts to be bonded toward one another. Create moments where people can truly feel like a ward family. Be mindful of the single sisters, widows, single mothers and the fatherless. Their hearts are especially heavy and they need the great fellowship that can be found in gathering with the Saints. Ask your Ward Council how to include less active members. Provide lots of mingling opportunities at your parties so the members can get to know one another better and develop stronger friendships.

For an activity to be successful you need to have the support of ward leaders. Attend monthly ward correlation meetings and involve auxiliary leaders in some planning so they will get excited and spread the word in their organizations. The more people you involve with assignments the more sense of ownership they'll feel in making the activity a success and the more help you'll be getting! Plan your calendar at least six months in advance. That way the ward leaders will see it on their calendars while they're planning and your events will be reinforced in their minds over and over again.

Talk with other wards to get ideas that worked well, share their decorations, and see if you can even create a Stake closet to store and recycle decorations. No sense in reinventing the wheel when you can just put your shoulder to it! Offer to help other groups with their goals, as well as provide fund-raising opportunities for the youth. For example, dessert at a ward party could be a bake sale or dessert auction with proceeds going toward helping pay for Scout Camp or Girls Camp. Coordinate with each of the auxiliaries to take turns preparing a musical number at each event.

Remember, you're not alone. Hopefully you have a committee full of enthusiastic people who also understand the spiritual nature of their calling. If not, ask the Bishopric to help you create such a committee. Include a "Spiritual Thought" during your meetings and remember that the people on your committee may be those souls most touched by your activities. Work as a team and brainstorm. If you let them choose the assignments they feel most comfortable doing they're more likely to complete them.

When writing out an agenda to pass out to your committee, be sure to include a section at the bottom of the page entitled "Action Items" where they can write down the specific things they are in charge of for the next activity. Thank your committee for their service after each activity and take a few minutes to review the good, the bad, and the ugly of the previous event so you can evaluate your committee's strengths and identify the weaknesses. Don't dwell on the negative, but seek to improve your efforts for the next event. You won't be able to please everyone all of the time, but if you're prayerful and try to magnify your calling, the Lord will be pleased with your efforts and His opinion is the only one that matters anyway!

Use the handbook that has been thoughtfully prepared for you by the Church. There is an activity planning sheet on the Church website that is another great tool for you to use. It can be found at www.lds.org/pa/images/ym/activityplan.pdf

Some items to consider while planning events with your committee are:

+ **Location**: equipment, decorations, A/C, entrances and exits, safety, parking, Plan B in case of bad weather.

+ **Time**: Announce specific start and end times and then follow through.

+ **Date**: Will it conflict with other stake, ward or family events?

- **Theme:** Coordinate decorations, invitations, refreshments, activities, publicity, posters, and music. Will it be uplifting or offend?
- **Publicity:** Be clever, fit the theme, be inexpensive, announce details including appropriate dress.
- **Decorations:** Consider the walls, ceiling, entrance, exits, food area, halls, bathrooms.
- **Refreshments:** Fit the theme, be creative, consider people with food allergies and other health restrictions.
- **Program:** Opening and closing prayer, mixers, entertainment, games.
- **Clean-up:** Assign specific people rather than hope everyone will just want to stay and help. Make it a game. Give thank you cards or small gifts to those who helped with all aspects of the activity.

This book is meant to be a big brainstorm of ideas. They are organized according to month, holidays and all kinds of national celebrations in the United States. Hopefully the suggestions will trigger your own creative brainstorm. Adjust the ideas on these pages to suit the needs and interests of your ward. Mix and match. The list is endless. Have fun and enjoy your calling! Before you know it you'll be released and wiping runny noses in the Nursery!

The twelve months . . .

Snowy, Flowy, Blowy,
Showery, Flowery, Bowery,
Hoppy, Croppy, Droppy,
Breezy, Sneezy, Freezy.

GEORGE ELLIS

CHAPTER 2

January

"It is deep January. The sky is hard. The
stalks are firmly rooted in ice."

WALLACE STEVENS
"No Possum, No Sop, No Taters"

JANUARY IS...

Celebration of Life Month

+ Plan a "This Is Your Life" event about the men in your Bishopric as a chance for ward members to better get to know them. Arrange for photos and mementos from their life to be displayed and invite their families to share funny experiences about them. You could play "To Tell The Truth" where the Bishopric tell stories and ward members have to guess which one of them is telling the truth. Tables could be decorated to represent different phases of life: baby, childhood, teenage, scouting, mission, college, marriage, career, grandparenthood, church service, etc. This is an especially fun activity when a new Bishopric has been called and you want to honor the men who previously served and introduce the ward to the new ones.

+ Learn more about ward members by inviting them to share experiences from their lives. Invite them to bring their baby pictures and see if everyone can guess which picture belongs to which name. Play the "Fact vs. Fiction" game where everyone has to share two things about themselves which are true and one which isn't; then the group has to guess what is fact and fiction. Check out Chapter 16 for ice breakers and mingling games to help ward members get to know each other better.

+ Back in the 1980s Kool and the Gang had the hit song "Celebration." It would be fun to kick off the new year with an 80s theme party, whether it be a dance, dinner, game night, talent show or whatever. It's a great song to remind us to celebrate the good times! Encourage everyone to dress in 80s clothing. Think Duran Duran, Miami Vice, Madonna, Valley Girl speak, Boy George, George Michael, the Eurythmics, and pastel Izod Polo shirts. Have a lip sync contest to 80s music and play some of the trivia games found at www.80s.com/games.html and www.inthe80s.com

Clean Up Your Computer Month

+ Decorate with a "Geek Squad" motif and invite people to learn how to do basic computer repair. Have someone give a short message on how to increase computer safety, firewalls, and protections that will help them "clean up" the spam and filth that often afflict computers. Invite your Ward Family History Specialist to show how to submit names for the Temple Ready program. Take a tour of the Family History Center and learn how to use PAF, Gedcom, and other computer resources. Encourage members to bring a name to prepare for temple work. Decorate boxes to look like computer monitors and accessorize with toy mice. Talk to your local computer store to see if they'll donate some prizes or supply guest speakers for a workshop. Best Buy would probably donate some "Geek Squad" T-shirts.

Creativity Month

+ Host a talent show where people can showcase their creativity. Set out tables where ward members can bring their handicrafts and projects to display. Set out a roll of poster paper where everyone can draw or paint something together. Paint a mural for the nursery. Put white butcher paper on tables so people can decorate the table where they're eating with their own artwork. Do a "Skit In A Box" by dividing everyone into small groups and giving them the task to come up with a skit based on the random items that are found in the box given to them. Have people design their own Pass Along cards or hold a contest to see which couples can come up with the most creative door approaches. Give small groups a box of craft materials and see who can come up with the most creative gospel-themed item.

Eye Care Month

+ Decorate with lots of eye glasses, sunglasses, goggles, etc. Invite a local optometrist to provide free screenings and share a short message about eye care. Watch a movie or play games that require keen eyesight like showing the group some items on a tray for a few seconds and then seeing if they can figure out which ones are missing when you take a few away and show the tray again. Serve foods that start with the letter I (eye) such as ice cream or foods that are known to be good for the eyes, such as carrots. Invite someone to share a message or entertainment about "seeing" the positive in others or keeping an eternal perspective.

Hobby Month

+ Invite everyone to bring items from home that represent their hobbies. Set out tables or booths where handicrafts and other projects can be displayed. Encourage people to dress in a costume or attire that represents their hobby. Have a talent show or set up stations people could visit to introduce them to various hobbies. Ask a local hobby shop to donate prizes or give out free samples of kits. Invite a local Hamm radio club, Karate school, radio control airplane group, or some other club to demonstrate what they do. This could be a great missionary opportunity for members to invite friends from their clubs to share their talents and interests with the ward.

Mail-Order Gardening Month

+ Throw a Garden Party, complete with fancy attire, white gloves, crumpets and other English formalities. Set out silk plants and flowers and decorate the room like an English garden. Invite musicians to perform and make it feel like spring in the middle of winter. Display pictures of gardens to inspire people to begin preparing their own at home. Have someone give a short message about how the Prophets have asked us to plant gardens. Invite a Master Gardener from your County Extension office to teach a class on how to prepare a garden.

+ Decorate with wheel barrels, shovels, pots, planters, seeds, silk plants and flowers, and other garden tools. Encourage people to dress in overalls and attire suited for working in the garden. You could even put people to use by having them work on the grounds of your building. Set out samples of sprouts for people to taste and focus on food that comes from the garden. You could show them how to create a pizza garden by planting basil, tomatoes, onions, mushrooms, etc., and then serve pizza. Set out a pretty display of potted herbs and have them taste different items using each herb. Play gardening games like tossing seeds into "holes in the ground" which are really cans or pots on decorated poster paper. Have people try to guess which seed turns into which plant. A neighborhood nursery might allow you to borrow real plants and flowers to set around the room for ambiance, as well as offer some prizes. Invite the Primary children to sing songs, dressed as flowers and plants that grow. Share a message about how our faith grows like a seed into a strong plant or tree.

Mentoring Month

+ Hold a Daddy/Daughter or Mother/Son event where families can bond and learn from one another. Set up stations where they can work on crafts, make refreshments, and play games together. Work with your youth leaders who will have some great ideas and who can be a helpful resource. Be mindful of adults without children.

Oatmeal Month

- Have a baking contest where all entries have to use oats as one of the ingredients in their recipes. This could be a breakfast where people sample all of the entries. Use farm décor with grains and grasses spilling out of decorated buckets and baskets. Roll out poster paper on the walls and have people add their own artwork to a standard farm design. Create a spa corner where members can see how oats can be used to make facial masks and soften the skin on elbows and feet. Have families make beanbags stuffed with oats to play various games.

- Help members develop a good New Year's resolution of bulking up their food storage by showcasing oats and all of the things that can be done with oats. Set out sealers where people could seal cans of oats for their families. Most Stakes have at least one sealer that can be used. Create a Taster's Table of recipes made with food storage items. You could even create an area in the building or parking lot where members help build storage shelves for each other.

Soup Month

- Have a SOUPer Social, of course! Invite ward members to bring all different kinds of soups, stews, and chili to share as part of a Soup Bar. Set out a variety of soup toppings such as green onions, cheeses, oyster crackers, bread sticks, French-fried onions, bacon bits, chopped tomatoes, etc. Provide a nice selection of breads and rolls, as well as some salad to round out the meal. Design decorations to resemble the classic Campbell's soup label. Use red and white gingham, aprons, whisks, chef hats and other kitchen utensils. Centerpieces could be made out of a pot with lots of different kinds of breadsticks and crackers spilling out. Invite the Primary and youth to sing and do skits. Play board games or work on a million different puzzles. Make it a cozy, fun evening. Have someone share a message or skit about all of the good things we "can" do to help people rid themselves of guilt over the things they can't do.

- Arrange for ward members to serve dinner at a local Soup Kitchen. They might be needed to serve food and clean up or else bring prepared sack lunches to pass out. Prepare some entertainment for the diners.

Staying Healthy Month

- Invite ward members to choose between several fitness classes held in your building such as aerobics, yoga, military PT, resistance balls, kickboxing, or karate. Then provide a healthy lunch or dinner, featuring a salad bar or low-fat versions of ward favorites. Set out a Healthy Snack Bar for samples of treats or Smoothies. Set small hand weights, jump ropes, and other fitness equipment on tables as décor. Have some races and outdoor games or get permission from a local high school to have ward members try various track and field events. Invite a personal trainer to share fitness tips. Invite someone to share a short message about the Word of Wisdom.

- Invite local doctor's offices, fitness centers, and even weight loss centers to set up booths and create a health fair for the community, offering free tests, screenings and samples. Call your local hospital for speakers who could present short classes about aging, back care, diet, exercise, etc. Guests could go home after having had their blood pressure checked, body fat levels measured, and other vitals looked at. Invite a chiropractor or masseuse to give complimentary neck and back massages.

Thank You Month

- Plan a special dinner party where ward members can invite someone they want to thank. Allow members to present a certificate and introduce their guest at an award ceremony. Set out tables with stationery, stickers, envelopes, rubber stamps, and colored pens so ward members can write letters of appreciation to teachers, friends, and family. It could be a formal event with speeches and trophies or a more casual event with fun entertainment and appreciation gifts. The ward could also invite city officials, firemen, volunteers from other organizations or people in the community whom the ward would like to publicly thank. What a great tradition and missionary opportunity this could be!

+ See more ideas listed under Thanksgiving in November.

January 1 — New Year's Day

+ Decorate with pictures of Baby New Year in his diaper, wearing a sash with the new year written on it. You could even use diapers as a theme to emphasize a new beginning. Play trivia games that reflect on the events of the past year. Award members with special certificates or prizes for accomplishments they had during the past year. Have the youth do a skit that reviews last year's events and silly predictions of what could happen during the new year.

+ Use clocks as a theme and review past decades in music and dance to showcase the history of our society. Decorate with a "Back To The Future" theme, mixing past events and future dreams. Divide people into groups and have them come up with funny skits of predictions that could happen in the new year. Create stations where people participate in activities associated with things like "Time To Dance", "Time to Sing", "Time to Work", "Time to Play", "Time to Pray", "Time to Serve", etc.

January 1 — Photographer Alfred Stieglitz's Birthday, 1864

+ Hold a photography contest where people submit their work before the event. Display all entries on easels or hang on room dividers to create a museum ambiance. Give each guest a voting sheet to choose his favorites. Decorate with all kinds of different cameras (real, toys, or made out of craft material) and put a disposable camera at each table so guests can take pictures of each other throughout the party. Develop the pictures to hang on your ward bulletin board later. Set up a camera station where families can have their pictures taken together in front of a pretty backdrop. Decorate in black and white décor. Display craft projects people could do at home with their photos such as decoupage a storage trunk or make a photo quilt. Create centerpieces at each table using wire or paperclips to hold photos of ward members on a decorative stand. Have children create a mobile, using photos of temples or their family members. Take a Polaroid picture of each child to use in a craft project for the parents. Frame pictures of temples, prophets, Church sites, or Christ for each child's bedroom, a husband's office, over a fireplace or other places of honor in their home or as gifts. Build frames out of beautiful wood or other interesting crafting material. Buy inexpensive frames and show fun faux painting techniques to dress up the frame.

January 1 — Betsy Ross's Birthday

+ Decorate with patriotic colors and colonial items. Create a ward flag or set up an area where families could design and make their own. Invite members of your local chapters of the Sons or Daughters of the American Revolution to provide entertainment, displays and speeches. Have someone dressed as Betsy Ross tell stories while children churn butter or work a spinning wheel. Take pictures of families dressed in colonial clothing. Set out a bunch of quilts that people can work on together and which can be donated later on. Learn about the history of the 5 and 6 point star Betsy Ross made and teach everyone how to make one at www.dltk-kids.com/usa/fold_and_cut_star_shape.htm A patriotic script is at www.gardenofpraise.com/heritage.htm

January 1 — Parade Day

+ Have your ward make a float to participate in a local parade if there is one. After the parade, invite ward members to stop in the building for breakfast or lunch.

+ Create your own ward or stake parade, encouraging families to decorate wagons, bikes or anything on wheels. Create a "Parade of Paper" by setting out stationery and stickers to encourage members to write thank you letters to ward missionaries, stake leaders, community service personnel, etc.

January 1 — Polar Bear Swim Day

+ Start a new tradition by holding an early morning swim in someone's pool or a nearby body of water. Serve breakfast and award participants with a special "Polar Bear Club" T-shirt. Decorate with polar bears, igloos, snowballs made out of Styrofoam, snow gear, etc. Have children build snow castles out of sugar cubes or Styrofoam blocks.

January 2 — Astronomer Isaac Asimov's Birthday, 1920

+ Using an outer space theme, put black poster paper on the ceilings and attach those glow-in-the-dark stars and planets. Light the room with black light and tell everyone to dress in white clothes so they'll glow in the dark. Create planets out of Styrofoam and build rockets out of appliance boxes. Have an alien-making contest by supplying participants with all kinds of miscellaneous objects. If you hold the event in the evening you could set up some telescopes for people to enjoy outside. Hang spray-painted cardboard stars from the ceiling and spotlight some of the "stars" in your ward by hosting a talent show. Make posters of astronauts and use a paper plate with a hole cut out to be the astronaut's space helmet. Serve samples of astronaut ice cream or other NASA freeze-dried foods which can be purchased online at www.funkyfoodshop.com or www.countdowncreations.com Paint a funny astronaut on a large refrigerator box so people can poke their faces through it to take pictures. Play a trivia game about the solar system and award winners with a Milky Way candy bar. Make sure someone sings the song "Fly Me To The Moon."

January 3 — Festival Of Sleep Day

+ Decorate with a glow-in-the-dark moon and stars hanging from the ceiling. Have lots of sheep on tables for people to count and a cow jumping over a moon. Asking people to dress in pajamas can be risky, so you could just encourage them to bring a pillow and wear slippers and a robe. Have silly contests like a relay that involves putting a robe and slippers on, putting rollers in the hair, speed-reading a bedtime story, brushing teeth, etc. Divide people into groups where they have to act out famous sleepy stories such as Rip Van Winkle or Sleeping Beauty. Children could come in their PJ's and watch a movie while resting on their pillows. Your theme could be "PJ's" which stands for Prayer, Journals, Scriptures." Did you know George Washington kept a prayer journal? Learn how to make pretzels to eat and share the story about pretzels and prayer: In about 610 A.D. a creative Alpine Monk decided to make use of pieces of dough left over from baking bread. The monk formed them into thin strips folded into a looped twist to represent the folded arms of children in prayer. This yummy treat was given to the children as they learned their prayers. They began calling the treat "Pretiola", which is Latin for "little reward." Soon it was known all over the world as a pretzel.

- Speaking of sleep, now is the time to start reserving your ward's spot if you're planning on doing a campout this summer!

January 3 — Author J.R.R. Tolkien's Birthday, 1892

- A Tolkien theme is sure to be a hit with the kids! Using the Lord of the Rings as your inspiration, turn your Cultural Hall into a forest. Avoid the really scary characters in the stories and focus on the brave, good ones. Cut out sword shapes from cardboard and have the children decorate their swords and use them to play various games such as tossing big plastic rings over castle turrets, also made out of cardboard or Styrofoam. Supply Hobbit costumes for the children and have them come prepared to sing or dance for the entertainment. Supply long white wigs and pointed ears for people to get their pictures taken, dressed as wise elves. Celebrate Bilbo Baggins' birthday. Take everyone on an adventure as they travel from room to room to participate in contests, watch someone dressed as Gandolf do magic tricks, write their names in Elvish, ride toy horses (or a real one!), or toss big plastic rings into a mountain made out of Styrofoam, make rings to wear, etc.

January 4 — Isaac Newton's Birthday, 1643

+ This would be a fun chance to host a science fair or create stations where members participate in weird science experiments. Make an apple piñata or one shaped like a light bulb to honor some of Newton's ideas. Go to www.nyelabs.com and www.stevesplangerscience.com to find clever science games and projects everyone will love. Learn about Isaac Newton at www.newton.cam.ac.uk/newton.html Decorate with science equipment (see if your local school will let you borrow some) and play games that emphasize gravity, such as dropping pennies into a small bottle while standing on a ladder. Wear a lab coat and invite a "Mad Scientist" to entertain.

January 4 — Trivia Day

+ Play Jeopardy as a ward and invite an "Alex Trebek" personality to host the show. Make up gospel categories, funny ones, or topics that poke fun at your ward such as "Holy Hometowns" (where people are from), "Alma Maters" (where people went to school), "Called to Serve" (Church callings), "Family Matters" (unknown facts about people), "The Best Two Years" (where people served their missions), "Talents Unplugged" (hidden talents), "Brother Doctor" (careers), etc. Invite ward members to compete as themselves or as famous people. Pass out a trivia questionnaire as people enter the party and award fake dollars for each question they get right. People can "buy" refreshments once they've answered trivia questions (make some easy so everyone can eat!). During the Jeopardy game have the youth or Primary perform short commercials for some funny entertainment.

+ With the cold weather outside, some people might really love a tropical party. Use "Gilligan's Island" as the theme. You can play trivia games to test peoples' knowledge about this old TV classic and have a costume contest to see who looks the most like the characters. Would you believe there is an entire web site devoted to helping you plan a party like this? Go to www.gilligansisle.com/party.html

January 6 — Bean Day

+ Sounds like a great opportunity for a chili cook-off! Decorate with a western or Mexican theme. You could also entitle the event a "Fire and Ice" party with homemade chili and ice cream competitions. Supply lots of small paper cups for people to sample everything in smaller portions, as well as some regular-sized bowls for people who want to commit to one kind. Supply chili toppings like sour cream, corn chips, tortilla chips, rolls, corn bread, avocado, chopped tomato, and cheeses. Put a sign next to each chili or ice cream entry and give everyone a ballot so they can vote for their favorite. Pass out "Golden Spoon" awards or blue ribbons. Invite guests to lasso a wooden rocking horse, decorate ponchos, make piñatas or maracas, and sing along to guitar entertainment. Invite the kids to have a Mexican jumping bean contest (whatever you envision that to be!) Set out samples of different kinds of chili peppers or hot sauces and have a contest to see who can handle the heat. Have people guess how many beans are in a jar. Play the "Bean Game" where everyone is given 10 beans to start. The person who is "It" says something he has NEVER done before. If anyone HAS done that thing they have to give "It" one of their beans. Go around the circle until everyone has had a turn to be "It." The winner is the person who has the most beans in the end.

January 6 — Epiphany

+ This could be a nice, short theme for a potluck or "Break The Fast" Sunday dinner. Teach your ward about this old Christian tradition that celebrates the arrival of the Three Wise Men. Invite your Gospel Doctrine or Seminary teacher to teach the true facts about the men who came from afar to worship the baby Jesus. Have your Bishopric dress up like the three wise men. Spray paint small rocks and herbs to look like gold, frankincense, and myrrh and place them in velvet-draped boxes for table decorations.

January 7 — Old Rock Day

✦ Go rock climbing as a ward and have a picnic. Okay, this is January, so it might be too cold for this where you live. You could decorate with an old miner's theme and send ward members on a rock-hunting adventure throughout your building. Spray-paint rocks gold to have them pan for gold with old pie tins. Build paths and rocks that children could safely climb. Encourage guests to wear overalls and dress like prospectors. Create a gold town by painting stores and buildings on cardboard or poster paper. Divide people into groups to come up with skits, using shovels, goats, cowboy hats, etc. Serve Pop Rocks and have the children paint "pet rocks."

January 8 — Elvis Presley's Birthday

✦ Have an Elvis look-alike and singing contest and decorate with lots of rhinestones, records, and Las Vegas or rock & roll memorabilia. Play musical chairs with Elvis music. Choose any of Elvis' hits as inspiration for décor such as "Jailhouse Rock" or "Blue Suede Shoes." Cut out cardboard guitars for children to decorate and have a lip sync contest. Serve peanut butter and banana sandwiches and Elvis' southern food favorites like corn bread, sweet potatoes and fried chicken.

January 9 — Aviation Day

✦ Celebrate airplanes by having a paper airplane contest. Invite your local radio-controlled airplane group to teach members about their hobby and have a chance to fly one outside. Set up the Cultural Hall to look like an airport terminal. Tie white helium balloons together to look like clouds attached to the ceiling which has been covered in blue paper. Set up various concourses where people go to get refreshments, play games like "Pin The Pilot On The Plane", and enjoy entertainment such as someone singing the Beach Boys song "Airplane." See an easy airplane craft made out of a stick of gum and some candy at www.kidsdomain.com/craft/plane2.html Create areas out of cardboard or poster paper such as an airport entry gate, gift shop, newspaper stand, etc. As the members arrive have them check in and receive a boarding pass, seat assignment and passport. Flight attendants could welcome them aboard and serve refreshments. Invite one of the Bishopric to introduce himself as the captain. Your airplane could land in various countries or you could have some of the young men in your ward "hijack" the plane and take it to various destinations. You could even have a spy from a certain country come and tell passengers about that country. (Be mindful of terrorist events that may make that idea inappropriate.)

+ Due to recent world events, the Church has asked that members no longer hold an activity where a plane crashes and then angels from each of the kingdoms of glory greet the passengers.

January 11 — Milk Day

+ Celebrate milk with an ice cream social. Provide lots of different kinds of ice cream flavors, drumsticks, cones, ice cream sandwiches, etc. Decorate with an old-fashioned milkman theme. You could even encourage members to bring their antiques as décor for the room or to have them appraised by a professional who is willing to donate his time and expertise a la "Antiques Road Show." Invite older members to share stories from bygone days and create a Barbershop Quartet from willing ward members.

January 11 — Secret Pal Day

+ During the holidays you could have ward members sign up to be Secret Pals with one another. Give them a month or so to exchange inexpensive gifts and anonymous service for each other and then hold a special event where their identities will be revealed. This could be a luncheon or dinner where people share their love for one another in speeches and entertainment. Decorate with a secret agent motif, James Bond style or Sherlock Holmes theme. Be sure to only sign up those who really want to participate and allow others who don't to gracefully bow out.

January 12 — Author Jack London's Birthday, 1876

+ Use his books as the inspiration for your décor and activities such as "Call of the Wild" or "White Fang." His fiction explored three geographies that would make for a fun party theme: the Yukon, California, and the South Pacific. To learn more about this author visit www.london.sonoma.edu

January 13 — Clean-Off-Your-Desk Day

+ This could be a career day where ward members share what they do for a living. Scouts of all ages and youth need to learn about other peoples' careers to meet "Duty To God" requirements, so this could be a productive activity as well as fun. Set up the Cultural Hall to look like an office with desks, water coolers, and work stations.

January 13 — Make Your Dreams Come True Day

+ Focus on Martin Luther King's dream and honor African American members in the Church. Create a ward time capsule for your ward where members write down what their dream is and plan to open it in one year or five.

January 14 — Artist Berthe Morisot's Birthday, 1841

+ Decorate the Cultural Hall to feel like Paris with a pastel impressionistic look in honor of this female artist. Play French music, eat French pastries, and set out paint palettes and canvas on tables for decor. Have teams try to build the Eiffel Tower out of various items and roll out poster paper where people can contribute their artistic talent to a mural for the ward nursery wall. Create an Eiffel Tower by covering a gigantic ladder with poster paper, drawing the outline and then stringing white Christmas lights either underneath or over the paper. Pass out a questionnaire to see if people can guess what various French words mean in English or see who can make the longest list of French words we use in English. Set out paintings on easels so that members can admire and discuss them.

January 14 — Full Color Comics Day

+ This date would be a great time to have a Super Heroes party. Encourage guests to dress as their favorite super hero and have a costume contest. Design creative contests where guests test their strength and super powers. Hang up signs that say "WHAM!" or "POW!" Give people capes to decorate and have them come up with a group skit about their powers and how they save the world from random, funny problems. Create an obstacle course, do face painting, and take pictures of people holding up a giant, Styrofoam globe. Remember, the Church discourages wearing masks at Church functions, so get creative with other parts of hero costumes. Be sure to include Super Heroes from the scriptures! Serve "Hero sandwiches."

January 15 — Martin Luther King, Jr.'s Birthday, 1929

+ Invite a gospel choir to perform and invite them to a dinner in their honor. See other ideas under January 13th.

January 16 — World Religion Day

+ This could be a phenomenal missionary outreach activity. Invite leaders and members from other churches in your community to join your ward for an evening of sharing, music and food. Allow each religion to be represented in song, dance, and speech and provide tables where churches could display items. Give each guest a copy of the Proclamation on the Family and celebrate the common values each of the religions share.

+ Help families learn how to keep the Sabbath Day holy by creating "Sabbath Stations" for guests to visit and then recreate later in their own homes. Each family receives a Sunday Box to fill with items from each station at the party and use on Sundays such as:

  Station 1: Make family stationery or letterhead with rubber stamps and stickers to be used to write letters to missionaries, relatives, servicemen, congressmen, etc.

  Station 2: Create and decorate journals and scrapbooks.

Station 3: Learn how to play a new instrument.

Station 4: Record the *Ensign* or scriptures on tape to listen to at home or to share with an older member whose eyesight isn't good anymore.

Station 5: Make Family Home Evening packets for future lessons.

Station 6: Repair the hymnals in the church building or some other service project.

Station 7: Make scripture snacks.

Station 8: Play scripture charades or do a scripture chase

+ Create a "Mission Possible" event where you send ward members on a "mission" to a different country. They could receive a letter in the mail before the activity, inviting them to attend and telling them where they have been "called" for the evening. Separate rooms can be decorated with items, music and food from selected foreign countries. Start everyone in a "Missionary Training Center" where a speaker could tell them all about their country and how the Church's missionary efforts are going there today. After spending time in their "country" they could then rotate through the other countries. Members could wear pretend missionary nametags and even be given a companion. Have a contest to memorize a scripture in a foreign language or see who can do the most creative door approach. A care package from "home" could be given to the members that includes treats and a sweet letter from the bishop. The mission president from your area could speak about how the work is going. You could invite the real missionaries from your ward to speak as well.

January 17 — Benjamin Franklin's Birthday, 1706

+ This could be a science fair, kite-flying party, or patriotic event. Have someone dress like Benjamin and share a message about how God blessed the American nation so the gospel could be restored. Decorate with old glasses, kites, patriotic décor, and old-looking documents.

January 18 — Hat Day

+ Encourage everyone to wear crazy hats and have a contest with goofy awards. Put snacks inside lined hats that are upside down on tables. Play games where people have to toss various items in hats or line up 9 hats to play Tic Tac Toe. Have children make paper hats or decorate baseball caps. Play Frisbee with berets. You could decorate with an Alice in Wonderland theme and focus on the Mad Hatter.

January 18 — Winnie the Pooh Day

+ On this date, Winnie the Pooh creator A.A. Milne was born in 1882. Have a big dinner like Winnie the Pooh and his friends had in the 100 Acre Wood. Decorate with beehives, honey pots, and balloons. Paint clothes pins yellow and black to look like bees and have people try to toss them into a jar. Invite people to bounce like Tigger in potato sacks to a finish line and invite everyone to search for a hidden Heffalump made out of cardboard in the building. Have children make a candy house for Eeyore out of graham crackers, pretzel sticks and frosting. Invite everyone to wear a red shirt to the party. Make a big cardboard cut-out of Winnie the Pooh and have people toss bean bags into a hole where his tummy would be. Serve teddy bear-shaped cookies and carrot cake for Rabbit. Thumb through one of Milne's books and you're sure to get a lot of cute ideas!

January 19 — Penguin Awareness Day

+ With the success of such movies as "Happy Feet" and "March of the Penguins" you're sure to find a lot of cute penguin decorations in the stores. Find a park with a nice steep hill where you can go ice blocking. Buy big blocks of ice and have the guests bring a towel to sit on. Create different heats of races so everyone gets several chances of competing against different people. Crown a winner and talk about Paul the Apostle's analogy of winning the race and fighting the good fight. Have people build igloos out of sugar cubes or Styrofoam blocks.

+ If you want to have a party indoors, decorate in black and white, snowflakes, icicles and Christmas wintry clearance items on sale in stores now! Have a "Happy Feet" dance contest. Have people stand on flat paper plates and then "ice skate" from point A to B in the Cultural Hall (if it has a wood floor.) Make giant penguins and snowmen cutouts of cardboard from furniture boxes and provide a selection of hats, scarves, colored markers, jewelry, and other accessories for party guests to decorate the cutouts. Make Rice Krispy treats round to look like snowballs.

January 19 — Popcorn Day

+ Have a Drive-in movie theater event with lots of popcorn and entitle it "The Reel Life!" Provide lots of big cardboard boxes, construction paper and markers so people can make their own car to sit in and watch the movie. Use a projector and a big white sheet on the wall to show the movie. Rent one of those popcorn machines and serve in movie theater bags or buckets. Ask your local movie theater if they could donate prizes, buckets or movie posters for décor. Make popcorn balls of different flavors or set out bowls of different spices and mix-ins so people can make their own popcorn concoctions. String popcorn to hang around the room. Divide ward members into small groups to film their own movies, supplying them with various props they're required to use or certain lines they have to say during the movie. Camcorders that record in DVD mode make it a snap to watch on a DVD player or computer in minutes. Award prizes for the winners in various categories. Have the Primary children sing "Popcorn Popping On The Apricot Tree."

January 20 — First Traffic Rules Published, 1900

+ Throw an "Anything On Wheels" event. Everyone is allowed to compete on an obstacle course or through various relays, transporting themselves on anything with wheels (roller blades, tricycle, skateboard, unicycle, scooter, etc) Invite someone from "Meals On Wheels" to talk to the ward about their national service organization and how they provide food to the hungry.

- Have a Pinewood Derby for the entire ward, using the equipment that the Cub Scouts use around this time of year. You'll need to pass out kits a week or two before this event so families will have time to prepare the cars. You could even invite some Cub Scouts to be the judges or to offer some tips on how to build the best car. Provide car refreshments by adding cookies to a Twinkie for wheels and add candy or frosting to decorate the car. Award certificates and include an "Anything Goes" category where there are no restrictions on weight or design and any car can compete. Have a short lesson on what we need to do to prepare ourselves well to compete and be successful in this life. Decorate with checkered flags, stop light posters, and toy cars on table tops.

January 23 — Handwriting Day

- This could be a nice theme for a potluck. Set out tables with lots of different kinds of stationery, rubber stamps, stickers, markers, pens, colored pencils, and gold embossing equipment for everyone to write letters to missionaries, military servicemen and women, and college students who are away from home. You could also encourage members to write a letter to their politicians to thank them for standing for truth and righteousness. Make a video of ward members sharing their salutations. Show members how to do fancy calligraphy. Set out painted wood blocks where people could paint their family name on as a home décor item they could keep. It would be fun to invite a local handwriting analysis expert to examine peoples' handwriting. You could also do it yourself at www.handwriting.org

January 24 — John Marshall discovered gold in California, 1848

- Have a fun Gold Rush theme. Try this fun audience participation skit by dividing everyone into groups that yell out a certain phrase every time they hear their name. Get old pie tins and go panning for gold (rocks spray painted gold.) Have a jug band concert where people make music by blowing into old jugs or stringing cardboard guitars, banging on pots and pans, etc.

January 25 — Opposite Day

+ Throw an Opposite Day Party where you do everything backwards, upside down, and opposite. Have a potluck dinner consisting of breakfast foods or serve a regular dinner but start with dessert first. Paint signs backwards. Perform a well-known play starting at the end of the story.

January 26 — Australia Day (Australia first settled, 1788)

+ Introduce your ward to the enchanting country and continent of Australia. Find some returned missionaries who served there to help you with ideas and to give a short presentation. Go to www.aussie-info.com to learn about the food, culture, music and traditions. Serve blooming onions and have everyone make a Didgeridoo and boomerangs. Set out some of those giant crocodile pool toys as decorations or for a wrestling contest. Set out stuffed koala bears and label the bathroom doors "Sheilas" (girls) and "Mates" (boys). Have a kangaroo hopping contest and dress in "Crocodile Hunter" attire. Divide people into groups to create skits about Australia and whenever they hear a buzzer or bell ring someone has to say "No Worries, Mate", "Crikey", or some other Aussie phrase.

January 26 — Wolfgang Amadeus Mozart's Birthday, 1756

+ Go to www.mozartproject.org to learn about this amazing composer and musician. It would be fun to have a very formal, Viennese waltz-inspired evening. Encourage everyone to dress in gowns and suits. Feature classical music and ballroom dancing. Invite the local high school orchestra to play or showcase the talents of ward members. Decorate with lots of velvets and rich colors, fine china, and pictures of Mozart. You could ask several families to "host" a table by bringing their nice table settings and decorations from home and helping out with their table. Offer a prize for the best table décor. Encourage ward musicians to perform some Mozart musical numbers. Cost Plus is a store that sells Mozart chocolates made and marketed in Vienna.

January 27 — National Geographic Society founded, 1888

+ This could be a nice theme for a potluck where people share food from around the world. Entitle the event "An Ensign To The Nations" and focus on recent Church magazines. Play games that test peoples' memory of past issues. Have the Young Women and Young Men present some of the messages from the *New Era* and the Primary could share items from *The Friend*. Work with your ward's Magazine Coordinator, if you have one, to come up with some fun ideas to get people thinking about how the Church magazines bless saints all over the world.

+ This event could be called "Dotting The Earth." Learn about the temples all over the world. As you display pictures of all of the temples you could design a quiz to see how many of the temples the members recognize and then share some facts about each one. Create a "Temple Trivia" game that members could play and then take home to share with their families for Family Home Evening. Invite some members to talk about different temples they have visited and have everyone place a white dot on a map of the world to show which temples your ward members have visited. Invite the temple president and his wife from the nearest temple to speak about the history of "your" temple. Help children construct replicas of various temples using sugar cubes, Legos, or building blocks. Using poster paper, draw the outlines of temples to hang on the walls. Invite members to bring their replicas of temples in clay, plaster, cross-stitch, crystal, wood, etc. Serve food from around the world and recruit the help of your ward's returned missionaries to gather decorations and share their experiences. Check out the beautiful temple kits available at www.lasting-fires.com

January 28 — Kazoo Day

+ Form a ward band by giving each of your guests a Kazoo and other simple instruments. Divide into small groups and have them learn how to play a song to perform for the other groups. You could combine this with a talent show and highlight people with actual talent.

January 29 — Puzzle Day

+ This could be a relaxing theme for a potluck dinner. Set out tables and chairs all over the room so small groups can work on puzzles together. Buy thick construction paper so people can design their own puzzles as well. Design a treasure map to a prize (dessert?) and then cut up the map into puzzle pieces that people have to figure out to earn the prize.

CHAPTER 3

February

"Why, what's the matter,
That you have such a February face,
So full of frost, of storm and cloudiness?"

WILLIAM SHAKESPEARE
"Much Ado About Nothing"

FEBRUARY IS...

American Heart Month

+ Have a heart-healthy activity with exercise classes and healthy snacks. Ask your local hospital, American Red Cross, or Fire Department to conduct a CPR class to help ward members certify. Decorate with lots of hearts. See more ideas later in this chapter listed under February 14.

Black History Month

+ Invite a local gospel choir to sing or perform traditional African songs and dances. Honor African American members in your ward. Show a Church video about the Saints in Africa.

Chinese New Year begins

+ Decorate with lots of Chinese lanterns made out of paper and tissue paper. Make a paper maché dragon head and have the Primary children do a dragon dance under colored sheets. Decorate with red and black accents. Check out www.asianideas. com for Chinese party supplies. Serve Chinese food with chopsticks. Set out Chinese take-out boxes with fortune cookies spilling out on tables. Find someone who can write people's names in Chinese on small poster paper for them to take home. Write "Gung Hay Fat Choy!" (Happy New Year). Find out what the new animal of the year will be and incorporate that animal in your decorations with lots of those stuffed animals and toys. Set out Chinese checkers games on various tables for people to play during the event. Your local Chinese take-out restaurant might be willing to give you a good price on chopsticks and fortune cookies that you could use during the evening.

Bird Feeding Month

+ Have children roll pine cones in peanut butter and then sprinkle with bird seeds for a bird feeder craft that could be hung from their backyard trees. Decorate tables with all kinds of bird houses. Guests could also make a birdhouse craft out of an empty milk carton by cutting openings on opposite sides and painting a design on the outside. For a perch, poke holes below the openings and slip a dowel through the holes. Glue Popsicle stick shingles to the roof. Fill the bottom of the feeder with birdseed. With permission, invite some ward members who have birds to bring them to display in the ward, reminding children not to touch. Set out bird-watching binoculars on tables. Provide a table with lots of feathers and have people make a bird hat to use in a skit about Tweety bird, Big Bird, Chicken Little, Woody Woodpecker, Woodstock, etc.

Cherry Month

+ This could be a nice theme for a Sunday "Break The Fast" dinner. Serve cherry desserts and have people dip cherries in chocolate. Have a seed spitting contest. Use real cherry blossoms in vases if they're blooming in your area. Set out cherry-flavored candies, Jello-O, jams, salsa, etc. Children could make cherry trees by making a handprint in brown paint for the trunk and branches and then dipping their fingers in red paint to add hanging cherries to the tree. Set out a table with the classic children's favorite board game "Hi Ho Cherry-O."

Dental Health Month

- Plan a fun potluck people could really sink their teeth into! Hang cut-outs of teeth and smiles all over the room and decorate tables with toothbrushes that guests can take home as party favors. Find a local dentist who will donate free samples of toothpaste and brushes. Use dental floss to wrap napkins around plastic silverware and to hang decorations from the ceiling. Have a dental health coloring contest and award prizes to the winners at the event.

Friendship Month

- There is a great painting by Pablo Picasso entitled "Hand with Flowers" that would make a colorful, simple theme for emphasizing friendship. Check out Chapter 16 for ideas on ice-breakers and games that get people to mingle and learn more about each other. Have people sit at different tables for each course of the meal so they get to converse with a lot of people during the evening. You could assign them a numbered table or just tell them to mingle. Have members bring different desserts and give arrivals a number that corresponds to the dessert they will be eating. Make friendship bracelets and pass out "Amish Friendship Bread" starters for people to take home and share with their neighbors.

Snack Food Month

- Plan a "Snack Attack" party and ask members to bring their favorite snack food to share. You're sure to end up with a lot of junk food, so prepare some healthy alternatives. Play games with snacks such as trying to toss Cheetos through a cardboard mouth, snack food trivia, Ding Dong hockey, M&M Tic-Tac-Toe, etc. Play games or make videos to watch while snacking.

February 2 — Groundhog Day

+ Decorate some tables to look like winter and others to look like spring. Use lots of weather vanes, mittens, scarves, and thermometers. Hang cut-outs of clouds, raindrops, and snowflakes from the ceiling and make snowballs out of Styrofoam. Give small groups various weather props for them to create a skit to perform for everyone. Roll out poster paper with different weather backgrounds so people can act out different weather-man skits. Find a stuffed animal to serve as your centerpiece groundhog. Play a trivia game from the movie "Groundhog Day." Children can make a cute popup craft by attaching a brown pom pom groundhog with jiggly eyes onto a Popsicle stick and sliding it up and down in a paper cup. Glue a picture of a groundhog on a toothpick and poke it into a donut or chocolate cupcake to look like a groundhog sitting on his dirt pile. You could also use the cupcake as his face and add two vanilla wafers for his nose and candy for his eyes and mouth.

February 3 — Artist Norman Rockwell's Birthday, 1894

+ The official web site for Norman Rockwell is www.normanrockwell.com where you'll find quotes, a biography, and plenty of wonderful artwork. Set up easels around the room to showcase some of the artwork by this beloved artist. Bring lots of props and divide people into groups to recreate one of his art pieces on stage as a kind of living art. Set out markers and crayons so children can try their hand at art. Decorate in an Americana-style with lots of home-made quilts and antiques.

February 5 — Girls and Women in Sports Day

+ Have a Sports Jam theme with games and activities from all different kinds of sports. Set out pictures of famous female athletes and honor the women and girls in your ward who are involved with sports. Hang a tire or hula hoop between two posts for people to throw a football or baseball through. If you're indoors you could have people play baseball with a plastic bat and one of those soft spongy balls. Before the party take pictures of various people in your ward. Cut and paste the faces (either digitally or by hand) and put them on pictures from the pages of *Sports Illustrated* magazine. Decorate the walls with the pages or use them as table top decorations. Have relay races using balls and equipment from various sports. Have a free-throw contest, using the basketball hoop in the Cultural Hall or creating a different basket for various ages. Play Frisbee golf, finger football, and induct people into a Ward Hall of Fame for goofy accomplishments. When people enter the party, give them a sports trivia questionnaire to fill out and turn in for refreshments. Encourage members to wear sports attire to the party. Families can decorate sports pennants to take home.

February 5 — Disaster Day

◆ What a great excuse to have an Emergency Preparedness Fair! This would be a great missionary outreach opportunity to invite your community to. Set up tables with displays, samples, demonstrations, and written material that guests can take home. Guests can wander around the booths or else you could divide people into groups that rotate through each station every 15 minutes or so. Have a station where people play Spin The Bottle and then have to eat food storage items when the arrow points at them. Show different kinds of 72-Hour kits in backpacks, rolling containers, #10 cans, plastic bottles, fanny packs, vests, etc. Show different kinds of water filters, camping stoves, tents, and first aid kits for car and home. Invite your local Fire Department to come and do a presentation. They have a great Smoke House they invite people to go through and all kinds of freebies for kids. Blockbuster Video will provide someone to do free identification videos and kits for children. Have someone show how to use a solar oven and offer samples of food cooked in Dutch ovens. Invite your local Hamm Radio Club to bring some experts who can share information and demonstrate their equipment. Your hospital would most likely be happy to provide a CPR class or information as well. Your community service office will also be a great resource for finding speakers and demonstrators. Find out what your community is doing to be prepared for a disaster and involve them. Talk to nearby Stakes to see if they have done a Preparedness Fair and borrow some ideas and resource material from them. Invite your local electric company to provide information on electrical and gas safety tips.

February 6 — Babe Ruth's Birthday, 1895

+ Have a good old-fashioned baseball game, of course! Serve hot dogs, Cracker Jacks, and peanuts in those brown paper bags used at ball games. Get permission to use a local field that belongs to the city or a school. Take pictures of everyone on a Polaroid and create baseball trading cards as a take-home gift. Encourage everyone to wear baseball hats and uniforms if they have them. Play a baseball trivia game. Design fantasy teams. Show a baseball highlights or blooper video. Set out a table where families can decorate their own pennant to take home. Award trophies to the winning players. In honor of the Bambino himself, serve Baby Ruth candy bars. Have a cupcake walk where people have to walk around an area decorated like a field while baseball music is playing and if they're standing on one of the bases when the music stops they win a cupcake that's decorated like a baseball.

February 7 — Author Laura Ingalls Wilder's Birthday, 1867

+ For inspiration go to www.littlehousebooks.com and www. littlehouseontheprairie.com Decorate the room to look like an old log house by painting a cardboard fence to go around the walls and creating a prairie feel with wheat in baskets, homemade quilts, and simple silhouettes drawn on brown butcher paper. Set out real logs or cardboard rolls painted to look like logs. Decorate with gingham and lanterns. Have people attend an old schoolhouse where the bishop speaks to them about reading out of the best books (D&C 109:7), and then have a picnic on the floor. Invite ward members to share musical talents and play old-fashioned games like hopscotch and jump rope.

February 8 — Boy Scouts Day

+ Recruit the help of your resident Scoutmaster for some fun ways to showcase the Cub Scouts and Boy Scouts in your ward. This would be a great outdoor activity, but if it's too cold in your area then you could set up the Cultural Hall to look like a camp site in a forest. Showcase the boys' talents by having them set up stations that ward members could rotate through, such as building fake fires out of pretzels sticks and rods, Dutch oven cooking, setting up tents, singing campfire songs, performing silly skits, knot tying, etc.

+ With the direction of your Scoutmaster, arrange for ward members to hold a big Merit Badge Day, offering classes to help the boys earn various merit badges. Use the talents and experience of people in your ward to help the boys advance towards their scouting goals.

+ Encourage the Boy Scouts and Cub Scouts in your ward to participate in National Scout Sunday by wearing their uniforms to Church. If you have a Sunday potluck after Church you could have them lead the ward in the Pledge of Allegiance and honor them with a special certificate and serve them dinner first.

+ Hold a ward winter campout. Supply lots of hot chocolate!

February 11 — Inventors Day and Thomas Edison's Birthday, 1847

+ Host a Science Fair or Inventors' Fair where ward members can bring their creations from home to display. Set up tables where guests can participate in science experiments and wacky contraptions. Give serious and funny prizes to reward everyone for their efforts. Serve a food bar (salad bar, taco bar, potato bar, dessert bar, etc.) so people can "create" their own food. Decorate with science equipment (see if your local school will let you borrow some) and play games that emphasize gravity, such as dropping pennies into a small bottle while standing on a ladder. Wear a lab coat and invite a "Mad Scientist" to entertain. Go to www.nyelabs.com and www.stevesplangerscience.com to find clever science games and projects everyone will love.

February 12 — Abraham Lincoln's Birthday, 1809

+ Design logs out of construction paper and have guests help build a cabin that could be taped to a wall. Set out Lincoln Logs so children can build log cabins. Play games using pennies such as a coin toss, Bingo (using pennies as markers), and a contest to see who can stack the most pennies without making them fall. Have President Lincoln "visit" your ward and give a speech. Your local Sons of the Civil War club would love to come and do a presentation in full uniform. See other ideas listed for Presidents Day on February 19th.

February 13 — Artist Grant Wood's Birthday, 1892

+ Grant Wood is most famous for creating the "American Gothic" painting of the somber husband and wife farmers holding a pitchfork. Use that image as your theme and encourage everyone to come dressed in plain clothes or overalls to take a similar photograph during the party. Use farm décor to recreate the look of old Iowa colonialism. Act out the song "Old MacDonald Had A Farm" and bring costumes to have groups create silly skits with farm animals. Paint a red barn onto poster paper or build one out of a giant appliance box. Set out bales of hay, milk cans and safe farm equipment. String a clothes line across an area and hang out overalls and funny clothes. Make pigs out of pink balloons and have a contest to see who can round up the most pigs with a fly swatter in 15 seconds. Go bobbing for apples. Set out some quilts people could work on. Serve corn on the cob and have children make dolls out of corn husks. Line terracotta pots with vintage material, tie a rope around the outside and fill with snacks to put on each table.

February 14 — Saint Valentine's Day

+ Throw a classic Valentine's Day party for everyone, being especially mindful of the singles and widows. Challenge guests to a Valentine's Day word search that they have to turn in filled out in order to get dessert. Tie red helium balloons to bags of hugs and kisses for the table centerpieces. Everyone can eat the candy as the night goes on and watch the balloons float up as the candy bags are emptied. Set up tables where ward members can display their wedding photos. As people enter the party, attach a card with a name or object on their back. They have to ask people questions about the identity and once they figure it out they have to then find the person who is wearing their "match." Create name card matches like Adam and Eve, Romeo and Juliet, Starksy and Hutch, Apple Pie and Ice Cream, etc. Freeze candy hearts or Red Hots inside ice cubes. Have a dance or lots of entertainment about people in love.

- Try a romantic Italian theme for Valentine's Day! Decorate tables with red and white checkered tablecloths and battery-operated candlesticks to recreate that dinner ambiance in the movie *Lady and the Tramp* when the two dogs eat spaghetti while listening to romantic music. See more Italian ideas in the index.

- Recruit the help of the Young Men and Young Women to serve dinner at an "Adults Only" fancy dinner. Dress them in black and white to look like waiters and drape tea towels over their arm. Help them prepare musical entertainment for the adults. Invite couples to bring their wedding cake topper to set on cakes for dessert.

- Host a "Loved Ones" Valentine's Day party and encourage the families to dress their members alike to take a nice family portrait. Set up a nice backdrop and ask a good photographer in your ward to volunteer her talents. Set out a lot of different kinds of candy bars or just those conversation hearts so people can design love notes and candy-grams to take home.

- Plan a family party for all ages but encourage people to come dressed as funny couples like salt and pepper, Sonny and Cher, Regis and Kelly, etc. Have couples play games together to earn points for refreshments and prizes.

- Plan a Valentine's Dance called "Dancing With The Stars." Hang glittery stars from the ceiling and drape Christmas twinkle lights everywhere. You could have a real dance competition or have some good-natured ward members plan to perform a funny, fake one modeled after the popular celebrity dance TV show.

+ Send adults and couples on the "S.S.Sweetheart" Cruise or "Relation Ship." Give guests a boarding pass as they enter the Cultural Hall. Set up beach chairs along the walls like on cruise ships and allow ward members to choose between ping pong, shuffleboard, volleyball and even a miniature golf course. Set up a fancy buffet table and "bar" where cruisers can go to eat whenever they want or else set up dining tables and serve everyone together. Decorate various "ports of call" in different rooms in the building or else in corners of the big room where people can go to taste food and do an activity like a game or craft. You could provide cruise entertainment and have your committee wear white staff uniforms with signs that say "Cruise Director", "Social Director", "Captain", "Doc", "Yeoman Purser," etc. Talk to your local travel agency and see if they'll donate posters, brochures, and prizes. Post signs reminiscent of the old hit TV show "The Love Boat" such as "The Lido Deck" or "Promenade Deck." Have someone share a short gospel message entitled "Anchored To Christ."

+ "Falling In Love With The Scriptures" is a love-laced evening that focuses on scripture study skills, testimony, music, and short plays from the scriptures. Set out tables where people can mark their scriptures, make book marks, write their testimony inside a Book of Mormon for the missionaries to give away, etc. Concentrate on the sermons of love that are taught and exemplified in the scriptures.

+ Invite another ward to join you for a Valentine's party or dance and advertise it as a "Double the Fun Dance" or "2 Fun 2 Miss" or "Twice As Nice!"

+ "Treasures of the Heart" is a casual evening of sharing where ward members can bring an heirloom to talk about as well as stories of ancestors who have inspired them. You could do an "Antique Road Show" theme and really focus on the older folks in your ward. You could play the "Newlywed/Nearlydead" game or "Newlywed/Oldywed" to be more politically correct.

Ask questions such as:

- What did you do on your first date?
- If you could describe your husband as a fruit what kind would he be?
- When your wife awakes in the morning what kind of bear would you describe her as: Grizzly, Polar, or Teddy?
- What is your spouse's favorite scripture story?
- What is your spouse's least favorite chore around the house?
- What color is your spouse's toothbrush?
- Name the hotel where you honeymooned.
- What is your spouse's favorite ice cream flavor?
- What is your spouse's favorite candy bar?
- Which spouse is more clumsy?
- Which cartoon character best describes your father-in-law? A.) Wile E. Coyote B.) Fred Flintstone C.) Homer Simpson D.) SpongeBob SquarePants
- Which one of the seven dwarves best describes your wife in the morning? (Happy, Sleepy, Grumpy, Bashful, Doc, etc.)
- Who received the last traffic ticket?

Award great-sounding prizes such as a brand new luxury liner (toy boat), a brand new Ford Explorer (Matchbox car), a brand new washer and dryer (sponge and paper towel), a brand new computer (calculator from the dollar store) or a romantic dinner for two (Spaghetti-O's and two plastic spoons).

February 15 — Gumdrop Day

- Decorate the Cultural Hall to look like the board game "Candy Land" by painting butcher paper squares on the floor. Design giant candies out of painted Styrofoam and cardboard. You could even have people play a human-sized version of the game by advancing to various areas and competing in games like a candy toss, making crafts or gingerbread houses with candy, designing bugs out of gumdrops, etc. Have a gumdrop flavor-tasting contest. Have someone sing the song "SWEET is the work" and talk about the sweet feeling we get when we live the gospel.

February 19 (or so) — Presidents Day

+ Decorate with patriotic décor and put snacks inside fabric-lined stove pipe black hats. Find men in your ward to dress as presidents Washington and Lincoln to take pictures with everyone and be greeters at the entrance. Paint a white house on poster paper, as well as scenes from history like Gettysburg, Washington crossing the Delaware or chopping down a cherry tree. Make giant coins and bills with the presidents' faces on them to cover walls and doors. Hand out a Presidents Day quiz that has to be turned in to get dessert or play a trivia game that includes questions about all presidents. Invite auxiliary groups to sing patriotic songs, do skits, read poetry or share short messages about inspiring presidents. When guests enter tape a card to their back with the name of one of our presidents. During the party each person has to ask questions to ascertain the president's identity that is on his back. Once they guess correctly they can win a prize.

February 25 — Levi Strauss' Birthday

+ This could be an easy theme for a potluck picnic or western hoe-down. Encourage everyone to wear jeans to the event and decorate with lots of denim. Decorate the space to look like an old-fashioned dry-goods store with barrels, crates, rocking horses, and buckets of industrial things like bolts and washers. You could even ask people to donate their old torn-up jeans and make a quilt, picnic blanket, pillows or tablecloths out of them. Put flowers or wheat inside boots as a table centerpiece. Hang a clothes line from two posts and drape jeans or long johns across the line. Have guests play a game where they try to toss items in some britches or pockets. Have a cowboy poetry contest. Encourage everyone to wear jeans or bring some to decorate with gems, rhinestones, fabric paint or fabric brads. Play horseshoes. Have a western BBQ or picnic.

February 27 — Polar Bear Day

- Have a Snowball Dance or "Snow Social" where everything is decorated in white twinkle lights, snowflakes and fake snow. Make snowmen out of big Styrofoam balls. Add glitter for extra sparkly snowballs. Hang snowflake cut-outs from the ceiling. Set up a real sled inside so people can have their pictures taken on it. Set out snow globes on tables and paint a winter ice skating scene on white poster paper rolled out on the walls. Have ice skating competitions for speed skating, short track and figure skating by making people try to skate on paper plates on the wooden floor in the Cultural Hall. Serve hot chocolate with lots of add-ins like mint chips, chocolate shavings, whip cream, marshmallows, and different flavored syrups. Make Rice Krispy treats in the shape of snowballs. Roll vanilla ice cream in coconut to look like snowballs. Play lots of "ice breaker" games from Chapter 16. Have people build igloos out of sugar cubes or Styrofoam blocks. Make giant polar bear and snowmen cutouts of cardboard and provide a big selection of colored markers, hats, scarves, and other accessories for party guests to decorate them.

- If you are really courageous, you could hold a ward Polar Bear Swim in an outdoor pool or pond. See the ideas listed under January 1.

February 29 — Leap Year every 4th year (occurring in 2008, 2012, etc.)

- Using frogs as your theme, play games like leap frog and have people make and decorate calendars. Decorate tables with cattails, lily pads cut out of paper, and toy frogs. Encourage people to wear green to the party. Have a croaking contest and see if you can find one of those motion detectors that makes the sound of a frog every time someone enters the room. Have a long-jump competition. See if there is a local school or nature center that has tadpoles and frogs that could be displayed. Serve green snow cones. For fun décor and prize items go to www.frogstore.com

CHAPTER 4

March

"Our life is March weather, savage and
serene in one hour."

RALPH WALDO EMERSON

MARCH IS...

Academy Awards Month

◆ Hold a fancy "Night At The Movies" where people have to dress
up and walk in on a red carpet (real carpet or else red poster
paper on the floor). Invitations and posters could look like
a movie ticket or be in the shape of the Oscar trophy. Make a
poster like a lighted marquee that says "Now Showing: The
Roswell Ward Movie Night" or other fun movie titles like
"Sister Shupe's Seminary Saga", "The Last Day of the Month",
"Attack of the Killer Jell-O Salad", etc. Cut giant yellow stars
out of construction paper to tape on the floor and have people
sign as they enter. Roll a painted sponge with washable paint
on each guest's hands and have them personalize their own
Walk of Fame star with a handprint. Hang posters of movie
stars. See if you can find some director's chairs to set out around
the room. Play games with movie trivia questions, "Pin the
Sunglasses On the Movie Star", or movie-title charades. If you
have cameras that flash without taking actual pictures you can
assign people to act like paparazzi during the event. Rent one

of those popcorn machines and serve Raisinettes. Find or make Oscar-looking trophies by spray painting toy figurines on a base and award them to random people in your ward for wacky achievements. Point spotlights and uplights on tables and focal points. Make giant white letters that spell out your ward name like the "Hollywood" sign in L.A. to hang on the wall. Have ward members divide into groups to make short videos that everyone can watch. Camcorders that directly record onto DVDs make it a snap to view quickly after filming. Encourage people to bring costumes and props and divide guests into groups that have to come up with a skit. To get their creative juices flowing, require them to use certain one-liners during their play or give them a theme. Hang drama masks on the walls or as table centerpieces. If your budget allows, you might consider purchasing a few silly (and clean) scripts from www.dramaticfanatic.com/products2. html Serve lots and lots of popcorn while the audience watches all of the skits. Award Oscar trophies to the best ones and have winners give acceptance speeches.

- If your ward gets a kick out of "Napoleon Dynamite" feature the characters and items from the movie into a fun party. Serve steak and Tater Tots served in Tupperware containers. Have a dance contest and eat "dang quesadillas." Teach sign language. Throw footballs and have someone teach "Rex Kwon Do." Encourage everyone to dress as their favorite character and give awards for the best costume and for the person who can say famous lines from the movie the best. Play a true/false game to see if people can guess which celebrities are Mormon. Find out at www. famousmormons.net

American Red Cross Month

- With the help of the Red Cross, organize a blood drive that can be held in your church building for the community. For more details go to www.redcross.org You'll need to provide volunteers, refreshments and some advertisement in your town.

National Craft Month

+ I don't know how excited the men will be about this activity, but the ladies will love it! Set up stations where people can rotate through to make various crafts. Provide supplies, plenty of hand wipes, some munchies and background music. You could offer estrogen-filled crafts indoors for the girls and more manly projects involving saws and electrical equipment for the brethren outside. You could have a theme for the event such as working on projects to help ward members with their food storage: building rotating shelves, making labels or storage charts, decorating storage boxes for the kitchen, building solar ovens, making aprons, etc. Home Depot, Lowe's, Michaels and JoAnn Crafts all offer free craft kits and for kids that they might donate for your event.

Frozen Food Month

+ Have an ice cream social, setting out all kinds of toppings for ice cream sundaes. Guests earn a topping each time they pass off an Article of Faith. Party guests could also create their own frozen concoctions by making ice cream sandwiches, Slurpies, Smoothies, and Cold Stone-style mixtures.

Kite Month

+ Have a picnic at a park and make kites and windsocks to fly outside. Provide kite paper for people to decorate, sticks, tons of string, fabric for kite tails, something for the kite string to be wound on, and lots of tape for broken pieces.

Noodle Month

+ It would be interesting to have a potluck and challenge people to bring only things that included noodles in the recipe. Well, you could relax that requirement for the dessert category. Children could make art projects with noodles and pasta or string necklaces and bracelets. Married couples could race to see who could eat one string of noodles the fastest while they each hold one end in their mouth (resulting in a kiss finale). Play "Pick Up Stix" with dried noodles. Have lots of brain teasers that make people use their "noodle." Have teams come up with skits that use those giant foam noodle pool toys. Have people write their name on poster paper using cooked noodles.

Nutrition Month

+ Invite people to bring only healthy food to share if you're having a potluck. You could do a salad bar or have a contest for vegetable side dishes. Play games that emphasize the food pyramid. Have everyone play games, make crafts, or do activities that earn them apple points that can be used to purchase apple pie for dessert. Ask a local health food store or farmer's market to donate samples or supply prizes. Invite someone to share a short message about the Word of Wisdom. Have someone dress up like junk food that the children have to chase away.

Play the Recorder Month

+ See if you can borrow some inexpensive recorders from your local elementary school and teach everyone how to play one, creating a ward band. Play simple Primary songs and then have a show with people sharing their real musical talents.

Poetry Month

+ Have a Poetry Potluck and decorate the party space to look like a cozy bistro where poets hang out. Encourage ward members to prepare something they could read to the group. Invite a few people to dress up like renowned poets and have them share famous poetry.

March 1 — Pig Day

+ Paint a red barn, fences, and farm scenes on poster paper to hang on walls. Set out bales of hay, corn stalks, and lots of farm-animal toys. Serve food in bowls that look like pig troughs. Have a pig-calling contest (Suey!) Children could make a piggy bank by decorating boxes or making paper maché pigs. Pig-out on ham, "Pigs in a Blanket," water chestnuts wrapped in bacon with a BBQ glaze, and pigs feet. Have a Pig Latin contest. Invite a few people to bring their Guinea Pigs to display and have the children play with. You could turn this pig party into a country hoe down with square dancing or clogging and go hog wild!

March 1 — Peanut Butter Day

+ This could be an interesting potluck theme with everyone bringing something made out of peanuts. Be mindful of anyone in your ward with peanut allergies! Have the kids play with Peanut Butter Play Dough. Play games like trying to toss peanuts into a particular container or "Pin The Peanut on President Jimmy Carter." Paint an elephant face on cardboard and then have people put one hand inside a long grey sock to be the elephant's trunk. See how many peanuts players can put in a certain container in 15 seconds. Play Jacks but use peanuts instead of jacks. See which group can spell the most words using peanuts. Be the first in a group to blow his peanut across a finish line. Show people how to crush peanuts to make peanut butter. Get the packing peanuts that are made out of a corn starch base and have people build sculptures by licking the ends and sticking the pieces together. Children can make peanut people by painting them and gluing those jiggly eyes on them, adding yarn hair, little hats, etc. Decorate with a southern peanut farm theme.

March 2 — Dr. Seuss's Birthday

+ Celebrate Dr. Seuss' birthday by having a breakfast and serving green eggs and ham. Encourage everyone to wear crazy hats or else they could make them there at the party. Go to www.drseussparty.com for all kinds of party supplies designed just for this occasion! Set out decoration vignettes inspired by Dr. Seuss books on tables and have people write down the names of the books that correspond in order to win prizes. Create Whoville by painting big appliance boxes like crazy houses and trees. Create an edible centerpiece using a Styrofoam cone that has cheese cubes stuck into it with toothpicks (cheese trees from "Fox in Socks"). Hang kites from the ceiling ("Great Day for Up") and stack stuffed animal turtles piled on top of one another ("Yertle the Turtle"). Hang pale green pants in your party room ("What Was I Scared Of?") and put large stars on the walls ("Sneetches"). Put a decorative weight on helium balloons scattered around ("Oh, The Places You'll Go!") and give people inexpensive Santa hats to wear ("How The Grinch Stole Christmas"). You could dedicate each table to one particular Dr. Seuss book as a theme. Divide guests into small groups to act out a book and provide them with lots of props. Children could make a giant stovepipe hat with red and white construction paper. Divide people into two teams (Thing One and Thing Two) and have them do silly relays like cleaning up a pretend house by placing items in a box, balancing many objects at once, tossing plastic fish into various bowls in 15 seconds, and other games inspired by the book "The Cat In The Hat."

March 3 — Alexander Graham Bell's Birthday, 1847

+ This could be a simple theme for a potluck by decorating tables with all kinds of toy phones and phone books. Play the telephone game where people whisper a phrase in the next person's ear to see how crazy the phrase ends up by the time it reaches the last person. Have a ring tone contest to see who has the most funny or creative ring tone on their cell phone.

March 6 — Artist Michelangelo's Birthday, 1475

+ Decorate with an Italian flair, inspired by Florence during the Renaissance. A spaghetti dinner would be perfect. Divide party guests into teams. Each team has a teammate with a basket tied to their head like a hat and their other teammates have to try to toss French bread into the basket from a certain distance. Have a sculpting contest where people have to recreate the David out of a block of Styrofoam. Children could make sculptures out of clay or play dough. Play a game where people are separated by a distance and have to really reach to transfer paint brushes to each other and paint a scene from the Sistine chapel. For fun you could have someone dress as Michelangelo, the Teenage Mutant Ninja Turtle, and walk around the room to visit guests. Make mosaics out of different kinds of pasta. Set out easels, canvas, painter's palette, smocks and other art supplies as table décor or for people to use.

March 11 — Johnny Appleseed Day

◆ Have an apple festival with lots of apple pie, apple tarts, apple cider, apple butter, apple/walnut salad, etc. Set out samples of different kinds of apples and have people vote for their favorites. Children could make apple crafts to give to their teachers at school. Crown an apple King and Queen of the festival. Set up games such as apple seed spitting, tossing apples into baskets, apple bobbing, and making crafts. Have people carve apple faces to take home and make dried apple face dolls. Decorate with apple garlands and wreaths. Decorate with a country flair and apple prints. Have a contest to see who can make the best hat out of pots and pans. Sing the song "The Lord is Good to Me."

March 12 — Fiesta de las Fallas (Spain)

◆ This is a crazy festival in the city of Valencia where the people build wooden and cardboard structures depicting various scenes and then light them on fire. While you don't want to host a pyromaniac event, the festival could give you a chance to introduce your ward to the wonderful country of Spain! Kids could play with sparklers and legal fireworks outside. Decorate with bulls, sombreros, flamenco dancers, fans, matadors, swords, and Don Quixote. Spain has a different culture from South America, so find a returned missionary who served in Spain to help you plan decorations and food. Children could make and decorate fans. Definitely serve Churros and flan. Teach everyone how to flamenco dance or dress children up as bulls and have parents toss a red cape or towel as the matador.

March 17 — St. Patrick's Day

+ Have a potato bar where people can top baked potatoes with cheeses, butter, chili, broccoli, green onions, tomatoes, bacon, sour cream, chives, grilled onions, etc. Sweet potatoes can be topped with cinnamon, brown sugar, white sugar, marshmallows, chocolate chips, syrup, butter, etc. You could also serve samples of corned beef, cabbage, and green Jell-O or have a potluck where everyone has to bring something made out of potatoes to get into the Irish mood. Legend says St. Patrick drove all the snakes out of Ireland, so kids could stuff long tubes of fabric and add eyes and a long tongue. See if there is a Celtic performing group in your area who could perform. Have everyone learn the Irish jig. Have a leprechaun trap-building contest. Advertise the contest ahead of time so families will have enough time at home to work on one they can bring and display at the event or supply a table of materials that people could use to build a trap at the party. Everyone who enters the contest gets a prize of chocolate gold coins. Get the Achievement Day girls to make posters of rainbows. Create a balloon rainbow entrance by attaching helium balloons at increasing heights and then arching down. Challenge each dinner table to come up with a funny limerick. Guests who wear green get a special chocolate gold coin. Have a contest where people have to cut a four leaf clover out of paper while their hands are behind their backs. Draw a leprechaun on poster paper and have the children play "Pin the Hat on the Leprechaun." Play "Hot Potato." Spray-paint rocks gold to scatter around tables and put in pots. Make a paper maché Blarney stone for the brave ones to kiss.

March 18 — Grandparents and Grandchildren Day

+ Decorate with antiques and hold an event that members could invite their grandparents to (if they live in the area). Your theme could be "Over The River And Through The Woods." Have children paint their handprint on dish towels to give to their grandparents. Take family pictures.

March 20 — Big Bird's birthday (He always turns six years old)

+ Use Sesame Street as your theme. Work with your Primary presidency to have the Primary children sing some songs and do skits. Have characters from the hit children's show make guest appearances. Decorate with a garbage can for Oscar, and make a giant Snuffy out of poster paper on the wall. Make big cut-outs of the show's characters that people can put their faces in to take funny pictures. Serve chocolate chip cookies for all the Cookie Monsters in your ward. Dress some people like Bert and Ernie and have them do a funny skit. Help Primary children or the Young Men and Young Women prepare songs and dances from the show. Sesame Street supplies can be found at www. partysupplieshut.com/sesamestreet/

March 20 — Agriculture Day

+ Have a salad bar and set out samples of all kinds of unusual vegetables your ward may not have tried before like jicama, okra, parsnips, kohlrabi, rutabagas, tomatillos, butternut squash, artichokes, fennel, etc. Set out lots of different kinds of veggie dips. Have people guess which seeds become which vegetables. Have relay teams shovel various items or use a small plastic watering can to move water from one bucket to another in a certain amount of time. Introduce ward members to "Veggie Tales" by decorating with some of the characters from the cartoons and reading one of their books. Set out different kinds of kitchen tools for people to shape vegetables such as radishes, potatoes, carrots and cucumbers and have a contest to see who can design the most creative artwork or sculptures.

March 20 — Pizza Day

+ Well, this one is a no-brainer! Have a pizza party! Set out all kinds of pizza toppings so people can customize their own pizzas or else serve different kinds by the slice. Get creative by introducing your ward members to chicken Alfredo pizza, bacon cheeseburger, BBQ chicken, Tai chicken, sun dried tomato and basil, veggie-style, Mexican pizza, etc. You could also serve pizza on different kinds of crusts like English muffins, Boboli, deep dish, cookie, French bread, Bisquick, deep dish, thin, etc. Ask a local pizza shop to donate balls of pizza dough for people to try to toss. Set up games that people play to win tickets that look like slices of pizza. Each ticket buys them a slice of pizza to eat or a topping to put on their pizza. Draw a giant pizza on poster paper on the floor and have people toss cardboard pepperonis onto marked spots to win. Cut out holes in a sheet or plastic tarp and hang vertically from two posts; players have to toss Frisbees decorated like pizzas through the holes to win.

March 21 — First Day of Spring

+ Celebrate the first day of spring by hosting a "Spring Fling." Set up gazebos, lots of flowers in pots and baskets, park benches, white wicker furniture, craft butterflies and ladybugs, and lots of pastel fabrics draped over tables, chairs and stage front. Find a Barbershop Quartet to wander around the room and sing to people. Encourage people to come dressed in fancy hats or else you could provide supplies and everyone could make and decorate a hat to compete in a contest. Serve a big salad bar, fruit kabobs and sprinkle tables with edible flower petals. Play croquet inside by poking metal arches into thick cardboard or Styrofoam so they won't hurt the floor. Have a strolling violinist or harp player perform while people visit and eat. Make giant flowers with a cut-out for a face for people to take silly pictures. Invite the Primary children to perform some songs. Have a modesty fashion show. Create relay teams where people have to fill flower pots with as many candies as they can in a limited time or transport a bouquet one silk flower at a time.

+ Using President Hinckley's "Way To Be" book, decorate with a bumblebee theme. Have a humming contest. Decorate with yellow and black balloons, beehives, baskets, and lots of craft bees. Set out lots of different kinds of honey for people to sample. Divide people into small groups to put together a skit, song, or presentation about one of President Hinckley's "Be's."

March 23 — Liberty Day

+ On this date in 1775, Patrick Henry declared: "Give me liberty or give me death!" Use Philadelphia as your inspiration for decorations and even food (Philly Cheese Steak). Dress someone up like the Statue of Liberty to walk around during the event. Decorate the party space with colonial décor. Have relay races where people ride stick horses and have to carry a lantern to a finish line. Children could put beans inside toilet paper tubes painted like American flags to make a firecracker shaker.

March 23 — World Meteorological Day

+ Design the room to look like a weather lab and decorate each table according to the four seasons of the year. Make folk art weather vanes, rain sticks, wind chimes, and sun clocks. Have a "Weather Man" be the host for the evening. Do fun science experiments.

March 24 — Family Day

+ Have "Family Home Evening 101" to help ward members get lots of ideas to help them with their Family Home evenings. Set up a room in the church to look like a living room and have a sample Family Home Evening with the ward. Set out a table where members can see all of the resources where they can go to get ideas for lessons such as the Church magazines, Sunday school manuals, the Internet, Gospel Essentials book, Gospel Art Picture Kit, church videos, and, of course, the scriptures! Have everyone prepare Family Home Evening packets with visual aids, copies of songs, recipe ideas for refreshments, suggested scripture reading, refrigerator magnets with scriptures or assignments on them, and copies of inspiring stories for all ages. Have families share some of their most memorable and successful family home evening ideas. Make different kinds of charts for FHE assignments such as refrigerator magnet displays, wooden houses with pegs to hang family names, simple paper calendars or elaborate computer spreadsheets.

◆ Hold a "Focus on the Family" event and invite a photographer in the ward to take pictures of families with nice backdrops to choose from. Have families make and decorate a family coat of arms for their home. Set up booths where people can learn about how to plan family reunions.

March 25 — Independence Day (Greece)

◆ Opa! Have a Greek festival! Decorate in white and blue colors, columns, ivy, statues, fabric-draped couches, pictures of sun-splashed white buildings and azure seas. Paint poster murals to look like the Acropolis and Athens. Encourage people to dress as Hercules, Zeus, Athena, or other Greek characters. Have a Taster's Table so people can try samples of Greek food without committing to a entire plate of something they may not like. For inspiration on Greek food go to www.greecefoods.com Mmmm . . . Baklava. Play Greek music and teach people to dance. Set out olives, hummus dip and pita bread wedges at each table. You could have an Olympic theme where ward members could test their ability in various sporting events to see who can go "Citius, Altius, Fortius" (Swifter, Higher, Stronger). Kids make catapults and have a contest to see who can toss stuff the farthest.

March 27 — Education and Sharing Day

◆ Plan a Teacher Appreciation dinner where ward members invite their children's teachers to honor them with a special award. Have Primary children and youth prepare musical numbers and speeches about how much their teachers have taught them. Decorate with apples, school busses, chalkboards, desks, rulers, pencils and backpacks. Some Stakes in the Church present a "Crystal Apple" or "Golden Apple" trophy and invite community leaders to help them honor educators annually. What a terrific missionary opportunity and service project!

March 30 — Doctor's Day

+ Decorate with stethoscopes, lab coats, ambulances, medical instruments, medical masks, funny X-ray pictures, etc. Make guests sign into an emergency room when they arrive and give them a medical bracelet and shoe covers to wear during the party. Make a centerpiece with an old-fashioned doctor's bag with first- aid supplies and charts. Set up a waiting room, fake operating room, cafeteria, laboratory, and gift shop that people visit during the party. Dress in scrubs and see if you can get a doctor's office to donate some of those paper clothes they make you wear to drape over chairs. Play the game Operation, have a medical scavenger hunt for items hidden in the building, and do "Body Part Bingo." Blow up medical gloves to make balloon decorations or have a relay contest with them. Have people race in wheelchairs. Give everyone a lollipop for being good patients. Hang signs for a Doctor's Hall of Fame such as Doctor Kildare, Doolittle, Frankenstein, Zhivago, Spock, Scholl, etc. Give everyone a prescription bottle filled with Skittles and a note that says how blessed we are to have the gosPILL in our lives. Have someone share a short message about the Savior as the Great Physician.

March 31 — Eiffel Tower Anniversary

+ What a perfect excuse to use a French theme for a party! See more French ideas listed in the index.

CHAPTER 5

April

"The first of April, some do say,
Is set apart for All Fools' Day.
But why the people call it so,
Nor I, nor they themselves do know.
But on this day are people sent
On purpose for pure merriment."

POOR ROBIN'S ALMANAC (1790)

APRIL IS...

Easter (sometimes occurs in March)

- Entitle this special celebration "In His Footsteps" or "A Walk With Christ." If your ward can handle a more spiritual Easter event rather than the usual Easter bunny faire, consider this idea. Invite someone who has traveled to the Holy Land to share photos, slides, and souvenirs from the trip and talk about places where Jesus would have walked. There are some great videos that show the sacred city and explain how the sites and remains have important significance to several religions today. Discuss prophecies that have and will be fulfilled in that land, current international events, and scriptures that talk about specific locations. With permission from your local CES Director, show the Seminary movie "To This End Was I Born."

- Have a Passover/Seder dinner. Talk to your local Seminary or Institute teacher for help in planning this activity that teaches ward members about the Jewish Seder and Passover symbols. It could be a full dinner or a Taster's Table with displays. A great web site is www.geocities.com/helenacan/writings/godly/ passover.html which has simple instructions for Christians who want to hold a Passover Seder, including recipes and basic explanations. Children could decorate their own Kiddush cup with jewels. Invite someone from a local Synagogue to sing some of the beautiful Jewish prayers and songs.

- Hold an Easter sunrise service with breakfast served afterwards. Check out www.marvelcreations.com/easter.html for Easter recipes, symbols, and poems. Serve Hot Cross Buns as a traditional symbol of the resurrection.

- Throw an Easter EGGstravaganza! If your ward is really hankering for a traditional Easter Egg Hunt then work with your Primary leaders to help plan fun activities for the children. Set up separate hunting areas for different age groups so the big kids don't run over the little kids and swipe all the eggs. If you only have one field area that would work you could stagger the timing when hunters are released by starting with the youngest children and then, after 30 seconds or so, invite the next age group to join them until everyone has had a chance to look for eggs and hidden prizes. Include a separate "Adults Only" Easter egg hunt with special prizes for them. Don't forget to hide a golden egg or two. Inside some plastic eggs the prize could be a slip of paper that dismisses them from clean-up duty. Invite the Achievement Day girls to fill plastic eggs with candy, toys and stickers. Relief Society sisters can donate colored eggs, and get the missionaries to hide the eggs. The actual egg hunt won't take long, so be sure to provide other activities. Hold an EGGceptional Bake-Off where people can enter their EGGstra special recipes to be judged. The only requirement is that the recipe has to include at least one egg.

Other fun activities for all ages are:

- Easter egg-bashing contest. (2 players bonk one end of their hard-boiled egg against each other. The egg that doesn't get smashed then challenges another person's egg. Last egg to remain intact wins.)
- Rubber chicken launch
- Egg decorating contest
- Guess how many jelly beans are in the jar
- "Pin The Tail On The Bunny"
- Relay races with eggs
- Raw egg toss contest
- Egg bowling (hard boiled eggs try to knock down empty water bottles)
- Egg rolling contest (mark a target and people try to roll their egg as close to the target as possible, like Bocce ball)

- Organize an Easter Cantata, inviting choirs from other Christian churches in your community to share music about the Savior. Provide elegant desserts afterwards and celebrate the common love for the Lord everyone has rather than focusing on differences of worship.

Autism Awareness Month

- Do a ward service project that benefits autistic children. Check out Easter Seals projects at www.easterseals.com For an inspiring idea, read about a Boy Scout whose Eagle Scout project involved making kits that help children with autism learn basic skills at www.stevecory.net/autism-info/AllenSmithEagleScout.html

International Guitar Month

- Have an air guitar contest or lip sync contest. Some areas actually have large competitions your youth could compete in! Amazing, I know. Invite someone to talk about how we shouldn't "fake it" in the Church, but live the gospel completely. You could also hold a real talent show and feature guitar players in your ward. Create a ward band by encouraging those old rockers to get out of the closet and perform. Each table could have a different kind of music for its decoration theme: country music, rock and roll, classical, blues, flamenco, etc. Kids could construct their own guitars out of guitar-shaped cardboard and then attach strings.

Keep America Beautiful Month

+ Do an outdoor service project. Check out www.kab.org Boy Scouts can earn the Hometown USA award by doing certain merit badges and an outdoor service project that protects the environment in their area. Talk to your city's Parks and Recreation Department to see if there are any projects your ward could help with. There is nothing like a good, dirty service project that binds sweaty members together and puts a song in their hearts.

Child Abuse Prevention Month

+ Work with your Primary leaders to plan an event that celebrates children. You could have a self-defense workshop and invite performers from a local martial arts school to perform and teach skills. Invite local child safety organizations to set up booths with information or offer classes. Have the Primary children sing.

Frog Month

+ I don't know which politician decided it was important to dedicate an entire month to frogs, but hey, it makes for a fun party theme! Play leap frog, toss toy frogs onto lily pads, and have Kermit the Frog visit your party or perform some musical numbers and skits with some of his friends from the Muppet Show. Serve green mashed potatoes, green Jell-O, green peas.

Garden Month

+ This is the perfect time to throw a garden party, indoors or outdoors. Have a flower show where you award winning flowers and plants with blue ribbons. Set out big containers of sand or rice where children can dig for wrapped candy pieces or inexpensive toys with plastic shovels and spades. Find a local garden store that will donate plants as door prizes. Call your county Extension service to find a Master Gardener in your area who could share his/her knowledge with the ward. The Extension office has pamphlets and great information on everything from lawn care to canning peaches! They can also provide you with kits to determine what your soil content is. Serve chocolate pudding in cups with crushed Oreo cookies as the "dirt" and Gummy worms spilling out of the cup. You could also bake cupcakes in small clay pots (check for safe ones first) and decorate tables with gardening gloves, pots, silk flowers and garden tools. Have a Taster's Table where people can sample different kinds of herbs. Share ideas and designs for planting a traditional English herb garden, pizza topping garden (tomatoes, basil, onions, garlic, etc), salad bowl garden, and other clever combinations.

Humor Month

+ Have a Stand-Up Comedian Night or call it "Open Mike Night" where people can tell jokes, sing, dance, or perform goofy talents.

Math Education Month

+ Play all kinds of number games. Have people make and bake pretzel dough numbers. Play "Are You Smarter Than A Fifth Grader?" Decorate the party space like a school room with desks, chairs, blackboard, pictures of school busses, backpacks, etc.

Daylight Savings Time begins

+ Entitle your event "Somewhere In Time" or "Stand As A Witness At All TIMES." Decorate with alarm clocks, watches, Grandfather clocks, stopwatches, and other time pieces. Invite ward members to create a Time Capsule either as families or for the ward or both! Give them a list of items to gather that represent their school, church, family, talents, friends, etc. Include newspapers, their written testimony, pictures, and their written "wish for the future." Put the contents in a labeled #10 can and seal (most stakes have a sealer for food storage that could be used for this). The cans don't have to be buried, but simply stored in a basement or closet until a designated time. Have families create a time-line of their lives on long butcher paper. Make a ward yearbook together with photos from past events.

+ Entitle the event "Spring Forward" and use the springtime ideas listed under March 21.

April 1 — April Fool's Day

+ Using a court jester's theme, play charades, have people try to say phrases with the letter "s" after eating a bunch of saltine crackers, throw whip cream pies at volunteers' faces sticking out of a plastic tarp, and have silly relay races. Put whoopee cushions on every chair and have an "Open Mike" invitation for people to share jokes and riddles with the audience. Give everyone those Groucho Marx glasses to wear during the event and to keep as a take-home gift.

April 1 — One Cent Day

+ Play lots of games with coins. You could have a carnival-style activity where people have to pay one cent either to attend the event, to participate in crafts or to buy refreshments. Hey, you might even make a buck! Using the faces of your ward members, create your own coins or paper money. Decorate with an antique motif with posters of things that used to cost a penny back in the "old days." Have an auction where people donate various items and all bids start at one cent. This could potentially be a fundraiser for the youth to pay for their summer camps. Play "The Price Is Almost Right", where people guess what old, random items cost at a thrift store or on eBay.

April 2 — Author Hans Christian Andersen's Birthday, 1805

◆ What a great excuse to host a fairytale party! Invitations and flyers could look like royal decrees. Invite people to dress up according to their favorite fairytale and include a contest with prizes to motivate them to really get into the theme. Invite a storyteller to read some of the books or get a group of people to act out some of the stories. Get Burger King to donate a bunch of their crowns to give to people to wear as they arrive. Make a "Once Upon A Time" poster at the entrance with "And They Lived Happily Ever After" written on the other side for the exit. Create a giant castle out of large appliance boxes to set up on the stage or as the centerpiece for your room. Using a small box, glue rounded paper to create turrets on the edges of a castle and color to look like stone for table centerpieces. Make princess hats by folding thick paper into a cone and attaching a flowing fabric piece to the top. Kids could decorate simple wands by wrapping ribbon around a pencil and attaching a big construction paper star at the end. Each table could be decorated with items from a different fairytale.

April 2 — International Children's Book Day

◆ This could be a simple theme for a potluck or dinner after Church. Invite people to dress up like famous authors or characters from their favorite children's book. Set up cozy corners where children can hear books being read by ward members. Decorate each table according to the theme of a different book. Have a book swap where people can exchange one new book for each book they donate. Invite a local author to speak or share a short message about literacy. Have children make bookworms out of pom poms or bookmarks by braiding yarn and attaching beads at the end. Since books contain treasures, you could have a treasure hunt, using clues from popular children's books. Wilton makes a cake pan in the shape of a book and most bakeries have edible paper you could use to look like pages on the top of the cake.

April 3 — Rainbow Day

- This would be a colorful theme for a potluck. Decorate each table with a different color. The Young Women will probably have tablecloths in different colors because of their Young Women values themes. Include Noah and the ark in the décor. Serve rainbow Jell-O or cake with different colored layers. You could hang paper raindrops from the ceiling and set out a different colored umbrella at each table. For tons of cute rainbow crafts check out: www.enchantedlearning.com/crafts/rainbow/ Roll out a large poster on the wall and have families put their painted handprints to create a rainbow design to hang in the nursery after the party. Set out a large pot at the end of the poster with gold chocolate coins for the guests to enjoy. Use different colored glow sticks underneath glass bowls or inside frosted vases to create pretty rainbows on tables.

- Decorate with a Wizard of Oz theme and be sure to have someone sing "Over The Rainbow" some time during the event! Tape yellow brick squares of construction paper on the floor in a path that leads from the entrance to a focal point such as the refreshment table. Make a rainbow arch out of different colored lights on a freestanding form. Decorate tables in blue and white gingham. Have the Primary children sing Munchkin songs while holding giant lollipops. Create a big hot air balloon out of appliance boxes and canvas fabric. Paint a poster to look like the Emerald City off in the distance and put flower pots of fake tulips in front of the posters on the floor. Have someone share a message about developing a heart, a head, and courage to do service or to live the gospel. You could also emphasize the importance of families and use the theme "There's No Place Like Home." Make little munchkin houses by painting appliance boxes. Tape pictures of ward members' faces peeking out of the windows. Make witches' hats to set on tables or float in a green punch bowl by taping a black party hat to a black paper plate. Set out ruby slippers or have people decorate tennis shoes with glitter, beads, gems, rhinestones, etc.

April 3 — Pony Express Established, 1860

+ What a great excuse to have a cowboy-themed party! Decorate with toy horses, cows, rocking horses, cloth bandanas as placemats, napkins, or tied around bowls. Set out cowboy hats upside down on tables with a bowl in the head part where you can serve chips and snacks. Play "Pin The Tail On the Horse" and create a lasso game where people have to swing rope around stuffed animals or a cardboard bull on a sawhorse. Paint old west town scenes on cardboard boxes and hang swinging cardboard saloon doors at the entrance to the building and bathrooms. Serve Sloppy Joes or hamburgers. Have a relay race, using stick horses and mail that has to be placed into various containers along a pathway. You could have a Hoe Down or teach everyone how to do country line dancing. You'll find all things "horse" from crafts to cookie cutters at www.colorofhorses.com

April 5 — Road Map Day

+ Decorate with lots of maps and toy cars. Hang posters that say M.A.P.S (Mormons Always Progress Shiningly) and a "map" of the Plan of Happiness that gets us back to Heavenly Father.

+ Create a "Road Show In A Day." Select a theme and divide the ward into small groups that each have to create a 10-15 minute show. You could provide props, scripture verses, songs or even certain lines that they have to incorporate into their skit. Everyone practices and prepares their performance for an hour or so. Break for lunch or dinner, offering a quick meal of some kind. Then everyone performs at night to your adoring audience. A great resource for tons of road show ideas is www.ldscn.com/ roadshow/

+ Create "The Amazing Race." Develop tasks small groups have to complete in order to move on to another area. This could be done in different rooms of a church building or actually out in the community. Some tasks could include a service project, memorizing scriptures, writing a skit, eating at a particular location, visiting someone, listening to a speech, etc. The first group to complete all tasks wins small compasses for being such great navigators and gets dessert first! You could also create challenges for the groups like cleaning various areas of the Church building, finding items in the building to create an Emergency Preparedness kit for the building to keep, etc. Another version of this kind of activity would be to play "Itty Bitty." Take pictures of items in the Church building but give the groups only an "itty bitty" sample of the pictures and they have to find the items.

+ There is a powerful activity used often for the youth in the Church, which could be tweaked to fit a ward setting. It's called "The Iron Rod." Re-create Father Lehi's vision of the tree of life by setting up a special trail the people will follow. Set up a long PVC "rod" which the members are told to hold on to during their journey while blindfolded. Using lots of cardboard, Styrofoam and imagination, have the guests walk past the river of filth, the spacious building, and other aspects of Lehi's dream. Have your committee members try to tempt ward members to let go of the rod, while others read scriptures and encourage them to continue. Once the members get to the end of the "rod" they can take their blindfolds off and enter a beautifully decorated room where they see a tree lit up and small white bags filled with special gifts.

April 6 — The Church of Jesus Christ of Latter-day Saints organized

+ Celebrate the restoration of the gospel by throwing a birthday party for when the Church was organized on April 6, 1830. Have people dress up like early saints to speak to the ward about what happened during the early days of the restoration. Play some of Joseph Smith's favorite games like stick pull and potato sack races. Play a church history trivia game. Serve birthday cake and ice cream. See ideas listed under July 24.

April 7 — World Health Day

+ Organize a Health Fair for your community. Invite local health and medical services to set up booths and offer information and freebies. Decorate with an international flair with flags and food from around the world. Go to www.fema.gov/kids/freebie.htm

April 14 — Webster's Dictionary first Published, 1828

+ This would be an easy Potluck theme to add some games and activities in addition to the eating and visiting. Play word games like Scrabble, Charades, Password, Pictionary (drawing charades) or "Scriptionary." Decorate tables with dictionaries, word strips, and Scrabble game pieces. Have a Spelling Bee and include funny names and words from the scriptures like Mahonri Moriancumr and Mahershalalhashbaz.

April 15 — Leonardo da Vinci's Birthday, 1452

+ Leonardo was truly the Renaissance Man who could do anything. Hold a science fair where people could submit their inventions or an art show where people can share their talents. Set out copies of some of his most famous art pieces and easels where party guests could try to recreate them. Create a mystery where people have to hunt for clues using Da Vinci codes. Make a big poster of Mona Lisa with a cut out where her face goes so people can put their own face in the picture and take a funny photo. Dress up some people in costumes to recreate the Last Supper in a spiritual or funny skit. For more ideas look at Michelangelo's birthday on March 6 and decorate with Italian flair.

April 15 — Tax Day

+ ANYTHING you do on this day will be a welcome relief to ward members who are stressed out from paying their taxes!

April 18 — Pet Owner's Day

+ Using a Noah's Ark or zoo theme, invite families to bring their pets to share. This event should be held outside for obvious reasons. Have a pet parade. Play "Pin The Tail On The Dog." Invite a local vet or pet store to share a short message on pet care or offer prizes. Set up obstacle courses for the dogs to compete in or hold turtle races. Provide lots of water for the animals, as well as waste bags and pooper scoopers. Children could decorate ID tags or bandanas for their pets to wear. Set out a table where people could make a "Trail Mix" for the pets by combining different kinds of dog or cat food. Have Scooby Doo "visit" your activity and offer Scooby Snacks to people and/or animals. Award "Best of Show" to one of the pets.

April 22 — Earth Day

+ Go on a nature hike with the ward or create one inside your building. Decorate with stuffed animals, hiking boots, animal footprints cut out of cardstock or printed on paper. Invite someone to share a short message entitled "Heaven: Don't Miss It For The World." Create a game where everyone has to guess which animal made various footprints. Assign the Cub Scouts or Boy Scouts to help prepare displays and games. Put pine cones in baskets around the room or set up a game where guests have to toss pinecones into baskets. Create large rocks made out of paper maché to set around the room. Serve trail mix, critter crunch (any mixture you want to put together), "Dirt" (chocolate pudding in paper cups with Oreo cookie crust on top and a gummy worm coming out of it), cookies or cupcakes with caterpillars made of M&Ms and animal crackers. Make a globe by painting a big Styrofoam ball and taping pictures of people in your ward to toothpicks standing on the earth. Set out recycling containers for people to bring their materials from home and use the money you get from their items to help fund your next activity or to purchase permanent recycling containers for your building. You can request free recycling boxes and labels at the website www.buyrecycledfirst.com

April 22 — Jellybean Day

+ This could also be a theme for your Easter party. Decorate each table in a different jelly bean color. When people arrive have them choose a jelly bean and that will be the table they have to sit at. Set out a jar full of jelly beans in one color at each table and have the people sitting there guess how many are in the jar. The winner gets to take the jar home. Give each table an assignment for a skit or song they have to perform. Have someone share a short message about how sweet the gospel is! Everyone has to answer questions to their table guests that correspond to a jelly bean color:

GREEN: What adventure would you most like to have?

WHITE: What accomplishment are you most proud of?

PURPLE: What lesson have you learned in life?

YELLOW: What is your pet peeve?

RED: What is a fun childhood memory?

ORANGE: Tell your favorite joke.

April 23 — William Shakespeare's birthday, 1564

+ Encourage people to dress in costumes from one of Shakespeare's plays and design a large cardboard focal point to look like the Old Globe Theater. Each table could be designed with items from a different play or set long tables end to end to create one gigantic medieval feast. Drape richly-colored fabrics and velvets across tables, chairs, and the stage with gemstones, goblets, and décor of the era.

April 27 — Arbor Day

Plant trees as a service project to celebrate Arbor Day. For a $10 donation, the National Arbor Day Foundation will mail you ten young trees that are supposed to grow well in your area. Planting and care instructions will come with the seedlings. Call 1-888-448-7337 or click on to www.arborday.org Decorate your party space to look like a forest with lots of Christmas trees (undecorated) and forest stuffed animals. Set up a few tents, fake fires, picnic tables and a pretend lake on the floor made out of blue construction paper. Kids can "fish" for prizes. Sing camp songs and do silly campfire skits. To request information and material to plant trees write to:

U.S. Environmental Protection Agency
Office of Public Affairs
401 M Street SW
Washington, DC 20460

CHAPTER 6

May

"Hard is the heart that loved
naught in May."

GEOFFREY CHAUCER

MAY IS...

American Bike Month

+ Invite everyone to decorate their bikes and tricycles and have a bike ride or parade around a park and then have a potluck picnic. You could decorate with a Tour de France theme. Before the event have people decorate paper and fabric squares to look like their bike sponsors that they can wear on their backs. Find a tandem bicycle for people to try or one of those bikes you pedal with your hands. Build an obstacle course for small children to ride their tricycles around. Show pictures of how bikes have changed over the years. Invite a local amateur team to give a presentation or teach bike safety.

2nd Sunday in May = Mother's Day

+ Talk to your bishop about what your responsibilities might be on Mother's Day. In some wards the Young Men and Young Women are in charge of preparing and presenting something to the women, while in other wards the Primary organization is responsible. Find out if YOU are in charge of this for your ward! Don't panic! There are plenty of ideas and you can always recruit help from the other auxiliaries. Here are some ideas:

- Have the Young Women and Achievement Days girls make bath salts, bath balls, or bubble bath that can be given to the mothers on Sunday. Their leaders will be happy to have a productive activity to help you prepare these.

- With the help of the Relief Society leaders, plan a pampering Spa Day for the women.

- With the help of the Primary presidency, plan a ward activity for the kids so that exhausted moms can get a break.

- Wrap floral tape around a pen or pencil and add a flower at the top.

- Wrap some gummy bears with a ribbon and attach a note saying "We could BEARly make it without a wonderful mom like you!"

- Ask the women in Relief Society what THEY would like. They may just surprise you and prefer that the money spent on them could rather be sent to the Church's Humanitarian Department or the Perpetual Education Fund.

- Wrap a soup mix with dried beans, veggies and spices in cellophane with a note attached that says "We think you're a SOUPer mom!"

- Attach a note to a small bag of Whopper candies that says "We think you're a WHOPPER of a mom!"

- Decorate small frames and take pictures of the Primary children and youth to put inside.

- Buy small containers of potted flowers to give to each mother such as African violets or pansies. Attach little hearts to sticks and put them into the dirt with a loving message or quote from the scriptures or Prophet about the importance of mothers. Wrap in polythene and tie it closed with a ribbon.

- Make chocolates or lollipops with candy molds.

- Make giant chocolate-covered Rice Krispy Square kisses.

- Make tissue flower bouquets.
- Make a pop-up flower garden card.
- Decorate votive candle holders.
- Make decorative soaps.
- Attach a note to a bag of M&M' that says "Me & Mom time is sweet!" or "You are a Marvelous n Magnificent Mom!"
- Make potpourri or sachets.
- Dip plastic spoons in chocolate, wrap in cellophane with ribbon and attach a note that says "A spoonful of love for you on Mother's Day!"
- Make refrigerator magnets with a nice quote about the importance of mothers.
- Make flower corsages out of ribbon. www.daniellesplace.com/html/mothersday.html
- Make recipe card holders.
- Make cute pin cushions made out of baby food jars and a padded lid with ribbon.
- Present them with a pretty bookmark with lace, ribbon or pressed flowers for her scriptures.
- Make a necklace hanger. Cut out a piece of cardboard into the shape of a heart and cover with batting and pretty fabric. Screw small hooks into the front.
- Present the moms with a pretty paperweight.
- Make one of those photo holders out of twisted wire and secure them onto a decorative weight made out of clay.
- Design heart-shaped brooches out of Plaster of Paris.
- Create a puzzle brooch. Spray paint puzzle pieces red or pink and glue in the shape of a heart. Glue a safety pin on the back.
- Make a flower coaster, coffee table decoration or paperweight. Arrange flowers in between two small pieces of glass. Wrap metallic tape (slide masking tape) around the edges.
- You can purchase some small Mother's Day booklets at LDS bookstores or else you could create your own! Have the Primary

children in the ward do the artwork and include quotes from Church leaders about motherhood.

+ Decorate small jars with a sign that says "Girls Night Out" or "Mom's New Dress" so the family could put their loose change in it so Mom can buy something she wants with it.

+ You can buy $20 gift certificates for See's Candy at Costco where you'll pay less than $20 for them. Then with those certificates go to See's and buy their little one-piece candy boxes to give to each mother.

+ Individually wrap chocolate-covered strawberries.

+ Buy six-packs of small flowers and transplant them into paper cups to give out to the moms. They survive a little better than if you handed each mother an individual carnation.

Bar-B-Q Month

+ Set up several grills from people's homes in the parking lot outside the Church building and assign the Elders Quorum or High Priests to do the grilling. You could also have a BBQ competition. Set out lots of different grilling sauces, marinades, and a Taster's Table for people to vote on their favorite barbeque sauce. Families could decorate aprons to wear and take home at the end of the evening. Decorate with chef hats, aprons, red and white gingham fabrics or with a western theme. Ask a local BBQ store to donate some BBQ tools as prizes. Introduce the ward to different kinds of grilled vegetables, fruits, seafood, and kabobs.

+ Have a Bluegrass Festival and cook southern BBQ with lots of ribs and southern side dishes. Teach everyone how to line dance or clog. Hang fireflies from the ceiling by making little construction paper flies and taping those glow-in-the-dark shapes to them. Decorate with quilts and built a little cabin with a front porch out of large appliance boxes. Set out some dogs on the porch. Decorate with wicker furniture.

+ A really popular theme for a BBQ event is called "Fire and Ice." It's a chili cook-off and ice cream social. Invite ward members to show off their favorite home-made chili recipes in a competition while the kids make ice cream with those old-fashioned hand-crank machines. Have people guess how many beans are in a jar. Have a chili-tasting contest, using different kinds of chili peppers to see who can eat the spiciest ones.

Better Speech and Hearing Month

+ Some Stakes have a tradition of a Speech Festival for their youth to improve their public speaking skills. You could hold competitions for all ages in serious categories such as expository, impromptu, debate, persuasive, dramatic interpretation, motivational, famous monologues, as well as fun categories such as after-dinner speaking, humorous interpretation, and stand-up comedy.

Flower Month

+ Host an "Everything's Coming Up Roses" Flower Show. Encourage ward members to bring flowers they have grown at home to enter into a flower competition.
+ Invite guests to create their own flower lei and tie it into a party with a Hawaiian theme. See ideas listed under May 1st.

Hamburger Month

+ Have a BBQ, featuring America's favorite fast food item! Serve French fries in different shapes and with various spices. Decorate with a 50's malt shoppe theme. Get the Young Women to wear roller skates, hats and aprons to look like waitresses at a drive-in hamburger shoppe. Set out a hamburger bar with all kinds of toppings such as: bleu cheese, BBQ sauce, pineapple, guacamole, cheeses, chili, Teriyaki sauce, onions, grilled veggies, mushrooms, pizza sauce, lettuce, tomatoes, pickles, etc.

Physical Fitness and Sports Month

+ Hold a "Ward Olympics." The original slogan for the Olympics was "Citius, Altius, Fortius" which means "Swifter, Higher, Stronger," so you could use a Greek décor theme. Spray paint cardboard circles gold, silver, and bronze to create ribbons for the winners. Cut giant circles out of colored poster boards to create the famous Olympic rings. Create a giant torch out of cardboard and red tissue paper (no fire is allowed inside the Church building). Display flags from different countries. Create an obstacle course relay, using various objects like chairs, tables, toys, silk plants, and whatever you can find to use at home or at Church. Have relay races. Award winners a gold-painted laurel or wreath to wear on their heads.

+ Have a sports game day where people can play Round-Robin badminton, basketball in the Cultural Hall, softball outside, bowling in the halls using sand-filled plastic pop bottles, volleyball, etc. Invite other wards to compete with or divide party-goers into small groups for tournament play.

Salad Month

+ Showcase different kinds of salads, such as green, fruit, pasta, potato, 3 bean, warm spinach, etc. Introduce your ward to a popular meat salad served in South America called "Ensalada de carnes." Provide a variety of toppings for a regular salad bar, such as sesame seeds, bacon bits, seasoned nuts, French-fried onions, cheeses, raisins, cranberries, dried fruit, croutons, etc. Have kids create animals, little creatures or flowers by using fruits and veggies. Families could cut designs into potatoes and make potato print designs on placemats.

Strawberry Month

+ Throw a Strawberry Festival! Crown a Berry King and Queen. Blow up red balloons and make little dots with a black marker. Make strawberry mice by putting two sliced almonds for ears and a chocolate chip for a nose on the point of a strawberry. You can use tiny squirts of frosting for eyes and skinny red licorice ropes for tails. Set out stations where people can do various things such as:

  + Dip strawberries in white and dark chocolate, caramel, marshmallow crème, etc.

- Show everyone how to dip a whole strawberry in sour cream and then roll it in colored sugar. (You can buy it at the store or make your own by stirring food coloring into sugar).
- Learn how to grow strawberries in pots.
- Taste different kinds of jams, jellies, syrups, glazes, salsas, etc.
- Eat strawberry pie, shortcake, sorbet, ice cream, tarts, or smoothies.
- Participate in relays carrying strawberries in spoons, etc.
- Make crafts out of those green baskets the strawberries come in.

Older Americans Month

- Hold a special dinner in honor of the older people in your ward. Decorate in a Roaring 20s, 50s, or even World War II motif. Set out baby pictures of the older ward members and see if the younger crowd can guess who they are. (Label photos with numbers and have people write down their guesses on a numbered flyer). Celebrate age by allowing the older people to tell stories and share their wisdom and experience. Play age relays where teams learn how to appreciate older people by walking with a cane, doing an obstacle course in a wheelchair, trying to see with blurry glasses, etc.

Transportation Month

- Have a ward car wash for the community. Don't charge anyone money, but give customers big smiles and a Pass-Along card.

Last Monday in May — Memorial Day (USA)

- Have a Memorial Day breakfast at a park and tell families to bring blankets and camping chairs. Begin the tradition of having the Bishopric cook pancakes, the Elders Quorum cook eggs, or whoever you think should do it. Make the chefs special patriotic hats or aprons to wear. Sing the theme songs from each of the military services: Army, Navy, Marines, Air Force. Give a plate of cookies, boutonnieres or small gift to all of the people in your ward who have served in the military to honor them. Invite them to share their experiences. Have a patriotic speaker share a short message. Decorate with everything patriotic you can get your hands on! Ask the children to bring their already decorated bikes and trikes or else you could provide them with supplies and they can work on decorating while the food is cooking. As part of your program, include a flag ceremony led by the Boy Scouts in your ward. Play outside games and set out a table where people could write letters to thank military men and women for their service. Ask ward members to bring items that could be included in care packages to soldiers overseas. Invite someone to play "Taps" on a trumpet.

+ With permission and planning ahead, have ward members meet at a military cemetery to place American flags next to each tombstone as a service project. Have orange juice, muffins and fruit afterwards in an acceptable spot nearby and honor any servicemen and women in your ward with a gift, speeches, and songs. See more ideas listed under Veterans Day on November 11.

May 1 — Hawaiian Lei Day

+ Here's your chance to have a terrific luau! Invite members of your Polynesian branch to attend if there is one nearby. They will be a tremendous resource for food, music and decorations. If there isn't a branch you might contact a Polynesian group in your community and they would be honored to help. If possible, roast a pig, grill teriyaki chicken, coconut shrimp or do a Hawaiian BBQ. If not, a simple taste of the islands is to serve Hawaiian Haystacks and lots of fruit. Have the Young Men and Young Women work on Hawaiian dances they could perform. Think Polynesian Cultural Center. Create grass huts by laying grass skirts over a small wood house frame or even a camping tent. Present party guests with a plastic lei when they arrive, or have them string their own at a table with lots of fresh flowers and leaves. Encourage everyone to come dressed in Hawaiian attire. Decorate with real or cardboard surfboards, skim boards and boogie boards. Create palm trees out of those big rolls inside carpet and attach real or green paper fronds. Have a cake walk with tropical music. Play the song "Tiny Bubbles" while a bubble machine blows. See if you can find someone who has one of those table-top waterfalls you could borrow and fill the room with lots of greenery. Set out beach chairs, a beach umbrella, and a little sand box at the entrance outside to let people know they're in for a treat. Have people do the Limbo. Serve fruit drinks with little umbrellas in them at a little bar created by resting a surf board over two stands. Have someone play the ukulele. Serve pineapple upside-down cake, macadamia nuts, fruit smoothies, and goldfish crackers. You could have people make grass skirts out of green crepe paper streamers. Make one of those standing cardboard people that everyone can put their heads through, such as a hula dancer or surfer. Provide each table with a grass skirt, straw hat, sunglasses, and wig and have the people sitting at the table dress a volunteer up in the costume and send him/her over to the stage to learn how to hula. Have a "Tacky Tourist" relay by making each person on the team take turns putting on a Hawaiian shirt, binoculars, sunscreen dollop on the nose and run to take a picture of something. Have a few men stand behind a chalkboard and pull up their pants to reveal their hairy legs. The audience has to vote for the best legs or their wives have to pick which legs belong to their husband. Find out what people's names are in Hawaiian at www.alohafriendsluau.com/names. html

May 1 — Mother Goose Day

- Decorate each table according to a different Mother Goose rhyme. Encourage families to pick their favorite rhyme and dress in costume. Play "Animal Sounds Bingo." Draw posters of Humpty Dumpty, Mother Goose, Bo-Peep, Boy Blue, Queen of Hearts, etc. Have each table do a skit reenacting one of the rhymes or the one their table represents. Make construction paper "pockets" to put flowers (posies) in on tables. Hang mittens from a clothesline and set out some stuffed kittens nearby. Make a big shoe out of an appliance box (for the old woman who lived in a shoe.) Use a stuffed white pillow case to create Humpty Dumpty and have him sit on a large painted brick wall made of cardboard boxes. Hang a cow, moon, and spoons from the ceiling. Play games that have to do with these nursery rhymes:

+ Jump over a candlestick.
+ Jump over a moon while mooing.
+ Carry buckets up little hills.
+ Toss spiders.
+ Have a relay to build London bridge out of blocks without it falling down.
+ Photo copy pictures from Mother Goose books and put a number next to each picture taped to the wall. Party guests have to write down the name of the rhyme they think the picture goes to.
+ Play Duck Duck Goose.

May 1 — May Day

+ Create a traditional May Pole by using one of the Boy Scouts' standing flag poles. Have everyone make flower garlands with colored tissue paper squares or real flowers if you can get a florist to donate some. Set out a flower press for people to learn how to make pressed flower bookmarks, stationery or another craft with dried flowers. Turn your cultural hall into a park setting with park benches borrowed from ward members. Make lamp posts out of used carpet rolls covered in black paper with flashlights in the top. Borrow silk trees and put clear Christmas lights on them. Most nurseries will loan you as many bushes and trees as you would like for the night if you just ask.

+ Using a Renaissance Festival theme, include a May Pole ceremony, jousting with wrapping paper tubes and stick horses, sword fights made out of cardboard, jugglers, etc. Serve chicken drumsticks and fruit kabobs. Invitations and posters could look like old paper on a scroll, using a flame to burn the edges. Decorate with lots of velvety fabrics, pillows, tassels, and rich colors. Have people create a family crest or shields by decorating cardboard or wood boards. Hang dried flowers and herbs from a metallic-painted potholder made out of cardboard or thin luan boards. Encourage people to dress as peasants, court jesters, knights, or lords and ladies. Levy a tax against anyone who doesn't come dressed in a costume. The tax could be to perform a song or joke for everyone. Hang tapestries on the walls or paint poster drawings to look like them. Create medieval doors and walls on poster paper. Kids could make sundials, soap, or candles in little shops. Have a town crier make silly announcements about random things during the event. Play "Pin the Horn On the Unicorn." Set up booths with burlap, palm fronds, and poster paper drawn to look like shingles. Find some people in the ward who play flutes to provide background music. Crown a festival King and Queen. For more ideas go to www.renaissance-faire. com

May 4 — Weather Observers' Day

+ Encourage people to dress according to the seasons of the year with a prize for the best costume in each season. Hang clouds from the ceiling made of paper, cotton balls or fabric. Make wind chimes, socks, whirligigs, or those cute umbrella hats out of colored construction paper.

May 5 — Cinco de Mayo

+ Can you say fiesta? Decorate the walls with a Mexican flag, maps of Mexico, Chihuahuas, posters of the country from a local travel agency, "Pin The Tail On The Donkey" (wearing a sombrero), and poster murals of a Mexican pueblo. Use candy-filled piñatas as décor during the party and let the kids AND the adults break them at the end of the party. Serve tacos, burritos, enchiladas, tostadas, tortillas, taco salad, refried beans, and Mexican rice. For dessert set out churros, flan and sopapillas. Put upside down sombreros at each table and fill with tortilla chips for people to munch on. Invite your local Spanish branch to help with food and entertainment. They would love to share their culture and talents with you! Cut out drawings of cacti for the walls and set some real ones on the floor and tables. Play Mariachi music and invite musicians from a local Mexican restaurant to perform. Tablecloths could be red, green or white with ponchos draped across for a splash of color. Encourage returned missionaries who served in Mexico to bring their mementos and share stories. Tie a red, green or white helium balloon to each chair. Have a pepper eating contest or set out samples of different kinds for people to try. Award a bottle of hot sauce to the person who can handle the hottest pepper without tearing up. Invite the Young Women to perform a Mexican dance. Have people guess how many beans are in a jar.

May 8 — No Socks Day

♦ Hold a 1950s Sock Hop! Encourage everyone to dress in poodle skirts, bowling shirts, leather jackets and 1950s attire. Create a malt shoppe or diner atmosphere. Hang old records from the ceiling and/or on the walls that can be purchased from thrift stores. Think "Happy Days" or "Grease." Serve hamburgers and hot dogs, ice cream sodas and floats. Have a hula hoop contest, bouffant hairdo contest, dance marathon or twist competition, bubble gum blowing tournament, and rock and roll air band concert. You can purchase inflatable guitars to use as decorations and for people to play with during the evening. Paint soda shop billboards and menus on poster boards. Using black construction paper, create large musical notes to adorn walls, hang from the ceilings and the back of chairs. Play "Name That Tune" using old 50's songs. Create an old Chevy from a large appliance box. Set out pictures of ward members who lived during the 50's. Make some of those stand-up posters of James Dean or "The Fonz" so people can put their face in the hole and take funny pictures. Encourage families to bring a pair of socks to donate to a local shelter. Have each family fill a sock with surprises to bring to the party in exchange for another family's filled sock. When families arrive they receive a number. All of the socks are set out on a table and given a random number. Hold up a sock and have the winning family come up to receive their prize.

+ Tell everyone to bring a new pair of socks to donate to a local charity. Have a "Flour Sock War" outside after a ward picnic. Fill old socks with about a cup of flour and close tightly with a rubber band. Remind everyone to wear dark clothes so that when they're hit it's more noticeable. Separate into two teams and let them go! You could play it like Dodgeball, Capture The Flag, or do several timed sessions like Paintball. When you get hit you are out. If you can play at a park that has some playground equipment, trees and bushes, then the players will have some shelters and can create strategies. Enforce the rule that no one can aim at another's head or he is out for good. Set out foot baths and find volunteers to give pedicures.

May 12 — Kite Day

+ Have a picnic at a park and make kites, wind-chimes, pinwheels, whirligigs, and windsocks to fly outside. Provide kite paper for people to decorate, sticks, tons of string, fabric for kite tails, something for the kite string to be wound on, and lots of tape for broken pieces. Serve sandwiches in the shape of a diamond with red licorice coming out the end to look like a tail.

May 12 — Ocean Day

+ Entitle your ward activity "Under The Sea" and convert your party space into an ocean by painting butcher paper with all kinds of ocean scenes to cover the walls. Use blue and green tablecloths, covered with fish nets and shells. Hang paper or plastic fish from the ceiling. Play "Sharks and Minnows" (without the water). Have kids fill water bottles with water, blue food coloring, plastic fish and shells, and oil to create wave bottles. Hide small toys in a big container of sand for children to hunt for (with a gigantic tarp underneath to protect the floor!). Serve smoothies and tropical drinks with umbrellas in the glasses. Serve coconut shrimp, popcorn shrimp, fish sticks, clam chowder, and chicken kabobs (for all those who don't like fish). Check out all of the fun water game ideas listed under August Water Quality Month.

+ Have a beach blanket BBQ at the beach (if you're lucky enough to live near the ocean). Make Bingo game cards on towels and play "Beach Blanket Bingo."

May 13 — Tulip Day

+ This would be a nice accent to a potluck or Sunday "Break The Fast." Find returned missionaries who served in Holland to speak about their experiences, display any mementos from the Netherlands, and help as a resource for ideas. Decorate tables with wooden shoes, little windmills, blue and white fabric, battery-operated candles, ivy, flower boxes, white picket fences, and tons of tulips! Have children paint their hand and stamp it on paper to create a tulip picture or attach painted egg carton sections to green pipe cleaners. Make a placemat for each person with a paper tulip flower that has an opening at the top for the napkin to sit, looking like more of the petal. Cut paper cups to look like tulips and fill with snacks at each setting.

May 15 — Restoration of the Aaronic Priesthood, 1829

+ Most wards have a great tradition of a Father/Son Campout. Invite a few speakers to tell the story of the restoration of the priesthood and talk about how the priesthood blesses our lives. Design the invitations or posters in the shape of a tent with flaps that open to reveal the information inside. Ask the Young Men or Primary children to sing some songs. Plan some outdoor games for the next morning after a pancake breakfast. Blindfold the boys and see if they can find their dads who take turns making funny sounds. A really easy breakfast is to pour a couple of raw eggs into a Ziploc baggie and drop into boiling water. Each person could add other omelet ingredients such as cheese, bacon bits, onions, peppers, ham cubes, etc. In only a few minutes the omelet will be cooked.

May 15 — Chocolate Chip Day

+ Throw a "Death By Chocolate" murder mystery dessert social. Set out a chocolate fountain, chocolate chip cookies, truffles, brownies, cake, etc. You can buy a Murder Mystery game out of a box at your local toy store that will consist of scripts you follow for about $30 or else you could design your own to include more people. Decorate with pink tablecloths and brown accents.

+ While the men and boys are off at their Aaronic Priesthood Commemoration campout, the women and girls could be enjoying a decadent chocolate festival and fashion show! Coordinate with your Relief Society and Young Women to help host this event!

May 19 — Neighbor Day

+ Host an Open House for ward members to bring their non-member friends to. Have each auxiliary set up a booth with displays and information about what they do in the Church. Have the Family History consultant give a tour of the library and present "The Gift of Family History" binder to help non-members get started. Create a few living room conversational areas with nice couches, chairs and rugs so people can sit and visit while they enjoy refreshments. Design an art gallery with pictures and sculptures of Christ, lit with up-lights and spotlights. See Chapter 17 on Missionary Work for more ideas on fellowshipping.

CHAPTER 7

June

"It is the month of June,
The month of leaves and roses,
When pleasant sights salute the eyes,
And pleasant scents the noses."

NATHANIEL PARKER WILLIS
"The Month of June"

JUNE IS...

Dairy Month

+ Enjoy a sports day outside and then treat everyone to an ice
  cream festival with lots of ice cream, shakes, malts, smoothies,
  sorbets, ice cream sandwiches, cones, etc. Have someone share a
  short message entitled "Got Testimony?"

+ Have a 1950s Sock Hop and decorate the party space to look
  like an ice cream soda shoppe.

+ Use a farm theme and decorate with a cow motif. Serve lots of
  regular and flavored milk, shakes and malts.

National Safety Month

+ Have a Safety Fair called "Take A Bite Out Of Crime" and invite
  the local Police Department to teach the ward how to start a
  "Neighborhood Watch" in their subdivisions and communities.

The Police Department can bring all kinds of pamphlets and material for the class, as well as provide fun things for the children that emphasize safety. Decorate with a dog theme, using ideas from McGruff the Crime Dog and the National Crime Prevention Council. Use yellow police ribbon to tape off sections around the refreshment table, games, etc. You can also invite your local Fire Department and county Health Department for additional resources, speakers, and handouts.

+ Introduce your ward and community to "National Night Out" which is meant to be a fun neighborhood party that focuses on no drugs or alcohol. (Perfect missionary opportunity!) Go to www.nationalnightout.org to learn more and to find out what resources they'll provide for your ward. Another great resource is www.nationaltownwatch.org You could begin a new tradition for your town!

National Fresh Fruit and Vegetable Month

+ Have someone share a short gospel message entitled "By Their Fruits Shall Ye Know Them." Have a Hawaiian luau featuring fresh fruit and veggies! See more luau ideas on May 1st.

National Tennis Month

+ Reserve the tennis courts at your local high school or community center and hold a tennis tournament for all ages. Create a round robin-style event so more players can play at the same time. Play tennis trivia games and have relays such as carrying a tennis ball on a racket for a certain distance or seeing which team can volley for the longest time. Have an air band concert with contestants using a tennis racket for their guitar. Adults could cut a slit in a tennis ball to serve as a mouth for a puppet and kids could decorate the ball with hair, hats, and a face to create a puppet show for the party. Invite someone to share a message about the game of "love and service."

First Week in June — National Fishing Week

+ If you need an excuse to have a ward campout near a lake, this is it! Tell everyone it's your national duty to celebrate by catching a fish or two. Recruit the help of the Boy Scouts and their leaders who may be involved with the Fishing Merit Badge to teach younger children in the ward and adults who may never have gone fishing before. Play a fishing game where everyone is sure to catch something, by setting up a wall or barrier made of sheets and have people cast out a toy fishing rod over to the other side where they can't see someone attaching a toy to the hook. Divide people into several groups and have them act out scripture stories that involve fish, such as Jonah or when the apostles were invited to become fishers of men.

Third Sunday of June — Father's Day

+ It may be your assignment to prepare something to pass out to the dads on Father's Day! If that's the case, here are a few ideas:
+ Make "Big Hunk" ties. Using grey cardstock, cut a rounded triangle shape that looks like the knot of a tie when folded in half. Glue ribbon in the fold and a Big Hunk candy bar between the open bottom halves. Tie them on to the fathers like a real tie.
+ Wrap several Treasures candies in colored cellophane with a ribbon and attach a note that says "A good father is a TREASURE beyond measure."
+ Make Sugar Daddy boutineers. By using floral tape, wrap the ends of a Sugar Daddy candy and attach either paper leaves or real ones so that it can be pinned on the dads like a boutineer.
+ Pass out small packages of Nutter Butter cookies with a note that says "There's Nutter Butter Dad than you!"
+ Make cinnamon rolls to pass out during Priesthood meeting with a note saying "You are so sweet, Dad!"
+ Take pictures of the Primary children and youth that could be placed into clear, inexpensive mouse pads for their dads.

- Make a booklet designed to look like a man's tie. Use several different colors of paper and cut each piece of the tie a little bit shorter than the last one so that it will look like a striped tie once stapled together. Under each tie flap write a different quote about fathers.

- Create a photo tie. Take pictures of the Primary children and youth and cut the photo to make the knot part of the tie. Cut out the rest of the tie on colored cardstock.

- Go to www.lds.org and check out the song "I'm glad that God chose me to be your son" that appeared in the *New Era*. Change the word "son" to "child" and invite the Primary children to sing it in Sacrament Meeting.

- Check out lots of Father's Day graphics and gift ideas at www. maryslittlelamb.com

- Make "Almond Joy" bow ties by drawing a cute oversized bow tie on cardstock and writing "All Men Are That They Might Have Joy" on it.

- Make big Hershey's kisses by using Rice Krispy Treats or chocolate and then shaping it in a funnel. Once they are cooled you just pop them out of the "mold" and wrap with aluminum foil, leaving part of a tag sticking out that says "Kisses to you on Father's Day!"

- Attach a note to a can of "Dad's Rootbeer" saying "We CAN hardly wait to wish you a Happy Father's Day!"

- Tie a note to an apple that says "Thanks for being the core of your family!"

- Fold paper into the shape of a shirt. Staple it close to the neck and insert a candy bar like Big Hunk or Sugar Daddy.

- Tie a ribbon and a note to a package of Pop Rocks that says "My Pop Rocks!"

- Put a ribbon and a note around some chocolate chip cookies that says, "Happy Father's Day from a chip off the ole block."

4th Week of June — National Camping Week

+ Have a ward campout. Recruit the help of your ward's Boy Scout Troop to help organize meals, supplies, and activities. Have a lumberjack theme with lots of flannel, trees, suspenders, and logs. Have a root beer chugalug, nail pounding contest, bucksaw contest, and tree climbing contest.

+ Entitle your event "Temples, Tabernacles and Tents." Help your ward learn about the Tabernacle in the Wilderness that was used by the children of Israel by having them help create a replica out of Styrofoam. Invite your Gospel Doctrine or Seminary Teacher to make a presentation about how it was built, the importance of the Ark of the Covenant, the staff of Aaron, manna, shewbread, the tablets, and other items that were contained within. Talk about how the children of Israel used it and what lessons we can learn from it. Create visual aids or a Family Home Evening packet that the members could take home to teach their families about the Tabernacle and the Lord's temples. Set up tents inside the Cultural Hall to represent the King Benjamin sermon when people gathered their families in tents to listen. Have someone stand on a ladder, dressed as King Benjamin, to share messages from the scriptures. Serve trail mix, S'mores, and set up fake fires built out of logs and red and orange tissue paper with a light shining from underneath.

June 1 — Donut Day

+ Invite everyone to share donuts and juice before a service project, hike, bike ride, campout, or some other outdoor event. Have a donut hole eating contest or hang donuts from strings to see if people can eat them without using their hands. You could decorate with a police theme (just kidding, Officer). Take a baggie and put frosted Cheerios in it with a sign that says "Donut Seeds." Teach everyone how to make donuts using recipes from www.recipes.lovetoknow.com/wiki/Category:Donut_Recipes Take some to the early morning Seminary classes the day after the party.

June 3 — Egg Day

+ Have a breakfast featuring Eggs Benedict, omelets, scrambled eggs, Sunny Side Up eggs, and every other way you can cook them. Decorate with those yellow smiley faces popular in the 1970s to tie in with "Sunny Side Up." For some "Have A Nice Day" smiley face trivia go to www.smileycollector.com/smileytrivia. htm You could decorate with lots of yellow and white, or use tie dye fabrics and turn it into a real 1970s retro motif, complete with hanging love beads, macramé, bell bottoms, headbands, and peace signs. Set out a table where guests can make pet rocks by adding those wiggly eggs and some paint or markers. Serve Tater Tots, Pot Tarts, Sloppy Joes, and quiche. Make Lava Lamp Bags by mixing oil and colored water in clear jars or baggies for the kids to take home. For 1970s culture and trivia go to www. funtrivia.com/Time/1970s.html and www.inthe70s.com

June 8 — Ice Cream first sold in the US, 1786

+ Have a good old-fashioned ice cream social where everyone can learn how to make homemade ice cream, using those hand-crank machines. People could also bring homemade ice cream from home to be entered into a country fair-style competition. Award blue ribbons for categories such as:

    + the most ingenious topping combination
    + the most colorful topping combination
    + the most creative name for their ice cream concoction
    + the flavor most likely to be adopted by Ben & Jerry's
    + the flavor most likely to be named after a Gadianton Robber
    + Best flavor
    + Best of Show

    Provide lots of different kinds of toppings such as bananas, brownie chunks, crushed Oreos, almonds, walnuts, peanuts, maraschino cherries, pecans, whipped cream, M&Ms, fruit, coconut, candies, flavored syrups, chocolate fudge, caramel, etc.

June 10 — Celebrate the birthday of author Maurice Sendak

+ Sendak's most popular book is probably "Where The Wild Things Are," so create a jungle theme by hanging vines, leaves, paper butterflies and stuffed animal monkeys from the ceilings and doorways. Decorate with safari hats, wild creatures, animal prints, bamboo, nets, safari boxes, drums, wooden statues, and grass skirts hung over wood frames or appliance boxes to create huts. Serve Grilled Boa (hot dogs), Water Buffalo milkshakes, Anaconda Delight (chicken), and fruit kabobs. Use coconuts to knock over half-empty water bottles for Safari Bowling. Recruit the help of the Young Women to do animal face painting. Create jungle scenery on butcher paper to line the walls and allow party guests to add their own animals and creatures to the mural. Have a lion-roaring contest and prize for the Most Ferocious Beast sound. Wilton has jungle animal candy and cake molds. Encourage people to come dressed in khaki attire and be ready for a hunt around the Church building for various animal scenes and items. Roll two black pieces of construction paper and attach to string so people can wear binoculars around their neck. Set out a fog machine, do the Limbo, make snakes out of long fabric tubes, and set out a lot of silk trees and plants. Invite Tarzan to "visit" your ward.

June 11 — Oceanographer Jacques Cousteau's Birthday, 1910

+ Have an "Under the Sea" party. (See May 12th.) To learn more about Cousteau check out www.cousteau.org

June 14 — Flag Day

+ This date commemorates when the official design of the American Flag was adopted by the Second Continental Congress. Invite someone to be Betsy Ross to speak and have the Boy Scouts do a flag ceremony and patriotic presentation. Serve Philly Cheesesteaks in honor of the Betsy Ross House in Philadelphia. With permission, have your ward put flags on tombstones at a military cemetery or around the neighborhood where your

Church building is located. Decorate cakes and Jell-O salads with strawberries, blueberries and whipped cream to look like flags. Make patriotic crafts to help families prepare their homes for the upcoming 4th of July festivities.

+ Teach families about the "Title of Liberty" story in the Book of Mormon and have families create their own family flag to hang in their homes.

June 18 — Picnic Day

+ Have a ward picnic at a nearby park and combine the lunch with kite flying, badminton, volleyball, giant bubble blowing, relay races, "Ultimate Frisbee," Flag Football, watermelon-spitting contest, "Capture The Flag" and other outdoor games. Offer plenty of prizes and Mixer games found in the Ice Breaker chapter. Set out red and white gingham tablecloths and decorate with an ant motif.

June 19 — Statue of Liberty arrived in the United States, 1885

+ Party supply stores have an inexpensive Statue of Liberty costume someone could wear to greet party guests. Since the statue was a gift from France, you could decorate with a French theme. Play a Statue of Liberty trivia game.

June 21 — First Day of Summer

+ Throw a Pool Party! This can be a party at an actual pool or indoors to give the atmosphere of summer fun. It's also a fun party idea to do in the cold winter. Draw diving boards on poster paper and lay them on the floor next to another poster you've painted blue to look like a pool. Decorate with towels, swim goggles, kiddie pools, floaties, beach balls, inflatable toys, sunglasses, beach umbrellas and chairs. Play Marco Polo with or without a real pool, water volleyball, and "Pin the Sunglasses on the Dolphin." If you're actually outside provide guests with squirt guns, water balloons, and sprinkler toys. Slip & Slides are great fun, but kids need to be monitored and the slide needs to be moved frequently so as not to kill the grass. Play Tug of War over a kiddie pool. Have a ward day at the beach if you're lucky enough to live close to one!

June 27 — The martyrdom of Joseph Smith

+ For a lovely, spiritual program consider "My Servant Joseph" written by Kenneth Cope. It's a Reader's Theater performance with four speaking parts plus a choir and some solos and duets. Set out pictures of Joseph Smith on easels with uplights underneath, arranged in between lots of plants, trees and park benches for a peaceful setting.

+ Recreate Nauvoo in your church building and have people visit different rooms where they can make a brick out of mud and straw for the "Red Brick Store", taste treats at the "Scovill Bakery", go "fishing" for a toy in the Mississippi River, make dough sculptures for the Sculpture Garden, dance, make Sunstone rubbings, sing songs in the Nauvoo Mansion House, etc. To learn more about the town and get ideas for your own version go to www.nauvoo.com or www.nauvoo.net Encourage ward members who have visited Nauvoo to share their experiences and photos.

CHAPTER 8

July

"The flames kindled on the 4 of July 1776, have spread over too much of the globe to be extinguished by the feeble engines of despotism; on the contrary, they will consume these engines and all who work them."

———————

THOMAS JEFFERSON

JULY IS...

Recreation and Parks Month

+ This is a perfect time of year for outdoor games, picnics, pool parties and Sports Jams. Call your city's Parks and Recreation office to see what facilities might be available for your ward to use.

Anti-Boredom Month

+ Have a "Board Game Night", by setting out all kinds of stations for crafts, games, sports, food, entertainment and mingling so no one will have an excuse to be bored! Play some music and have everyone go to the table of their choice and start playing the game when the music stops. When they hear music playing again (after 10 or 15 minutes) they have to pick a winner and run to another table to play a different board game. Set up a giant Tic Toe Toe square on the floor marked with tape and have the people be the game pieces. Decorate with game pieces, Monopoly money, battleships, puzzles, and giant dice made out of big boxes. This would be a good party theme for those cold, winter months when you're stuck inside! Use black lights in the room to make everything glow. Give everyone glow-in-the-dark bracelets to wear. Spray a beach ball with glow in the dark paint or squirt some of the glow-in-the-dark liquid from those sticks inside the beach ball and play Glow-In-The-Dark volleyball.

Anytime in July — Green Corn Celebration by Seminoles

+ Have an Indian Pow Wow! Kids could make beaded necklaces or decorate totem poles made out of paper towel cardboard tubes. Serve Navajo Tacos. To learn more about this festival and dance check out www.brownielocks.com/greencorndance.html

July 4 — Independence Day

+ People are always in the mood for a great BBQ or picnic on this day. Have Uncle Sam or Thomas Jefferson visit your ward to give a patriotic speech or read aloud the Declaration of Independence. To find good material go to www.ushistory.org/declaration Invite the Boy Scouts to do a flag ceremony at the beginning and end of your event. Sing patriotic songs found at www. patrioticon.org/patriotic-soundfileslyrics.htm Have plenty of patriotic crafts which can be found at www.enchantedlearning. com/crafts/patriotic Set out a jar with blue and red candies for party goers to guess how many are inside. Have a U.S. history trivia contest, and set out patriotic games such as tossing red, white, and blue bean bags into a liberty bell-shaped container or toss rings around a Statue of Liberty torch. Set out lots of decorations for the kids to adorn their bikes, trikes, scooters, drums, and wagons, and then have a parade. Play patriotic music and have a relay race where people pass a small flag to team mates. Launch model rockets and award prizes for the one that goes the highest or bombs the worst. Decorate cakes, cupcakes, and

Jell-O with strawberries, whip cream, and blueberries to look like the American flag. Sing the theme songs of each branch of the military, read quotes from famous Americans, and be sure to pass out patriotic stationery so ward members can write letters to our servicemen and women stationed overseas. Have everyone bring a white T-shirt to decorate with fabric paints in a patriotic design. Kids could make toy firecrackers by decorating toilet paper rolls and taping crackly ribbons to the end.

+ Serve a pancake breakfast so people will have time to enjoy their other festivities with families and neighbors during the day.

July 4 — National Country Music Day

+ Have an old-fashioned Country Fair. Decorate with lots of gingham fabrics and raffia. Have ward members bring various dishes to be judged for blue ribbon prizes. Encourage guests to display their handicraft items and create contest categories such as quilting, knitting, crocheting, woodwork, metal work, jewelry, artwork, sculpture, sewing, etc. See if you can find some information and discount coupons to offer for any county fairs going on in your area. Scatter stuffed animal pigs and cows for the obligatory livestock booths at the fair. Have everyone learn how to clog, square dance, or line dance. Set out decorative baskets of wheat, mason jars with raffia bows and snacks inside. Turn cowboy hats upside down on tables, and line the inside head part before filling with snacks. Encourage people to share their musical talents, especially with the guitar or banjo. Teach people how to play the jaw-harp, the spoons, and the kazoo.

July 5 — Caribbean Day

+ Use the popular movie "Pirates of the Caribbean" as your inspiration. Decorate in exotic island décor with lots of pirates, chocolate and plastic gold coins, gemstones and costume jewelry, treasure maps, buccaneers, and ships. Spray paint boxes of wood or cardboard black and brown and paint on silver locks to look like a pirate treasure chest. The invitations and posters could look like a treasure map, with "X" marking the spot for the party location. Use yellow paper and burn off the edges with a match to make it look old. Set out a 2 x 4 for children to "walk the plank" or as an entrance to the refreshments area. Serve goldfish crackers in shells on the tables. Have someone share a message about "talents to treasure" or "treasures in heaven."

+ Using a jungle theme create a "Survivor" event to emphasize teamwork and a few emergency preparedness skills. Divide people into teams and have them create a name, flag, and matching "buffs" to wear. Challenge them to create a shelter using only items they can find in the building. Play Tug of War, eat yucky stuff like raw onions, cooked liver, honey on tuna fish, etc. Give them "tree mail" where they'll get clues to find various items such as a blanket, water bottles, Trail Mix, etc. Play a survival trivia game. There is a great "Worse Case Scenario" book series which has also been turned into a board game that you can use to see how well prepared the members are. Win immunity for the team if anyone actually has a 72-hour kit in their car in the parking lot. Make fake torches out of dowels and red tissue paper. Have someone share a short message entitled "Seek To Thrive, Not Just Survive" or "It's A Jungle Out There", or "Hold Your Torches High" to emphasize the importance of the gospel in our lives.

July 5 — Family Day

+ What a perfect time to have a Family History Fair! See ideas listed on page 111.

July 6 — Fried Chicken Day

+ Decorate with a southern flair and a few rubber chickens. Make everyone talk with southern accents. Serve fried chicken, of course! Have a "Colonial" visit. Think Kentucky Fried Chicken. This could be a cute theme for a picnic.

July 7 — Macaroni Day

+ Decorate with an Italian flair. Have kids use dried macaroni noodles to make various craft items such as a frame, an ornament, a self-portrait or a temple.

July 10 — Teddy Bear's Picnic Day

+ This would be a cute theme for a ward picnic inside or outside. Cut simple bear shapes out of inexpensive fabric or felt for the children to sew with yarn and stuff like "Build A Bear." Serve those yummy cinnamon bear candies and have people guess how many Teddy Grahams are inside a jar. Play Hot Potato but use a teddy bear. Play volleyball but use a teddy bear that people have to toss over by holding ends of a towel. Do an "Over and Under" relay, moving a bear from the front of the line to the back and alternating over people's heads and under their legs. Divide people into groups and have them perform "Twisted Fairytale" skits, changing the scenes in "Goldilocks and the Three Bears", "Winnie The Pooh" and other stories that involve bears. Decorate with lots of different kinds of bears and maybe even a nature/camping theme so the men will find something masculine about the theme! This could also be a special Mother/Daughter event.

July 11 — Cheer Up the Lonely Day

+ Have your ward members visit a children's hospital or nursing home to perform songs, dances, and acts of kindness. Ask the Primary children to bring decorated cards from home. Sisters could paint fingernails of the residents and brethren could bring pets for the patients to hold. Bring a Polaroid camera to take instant pictures to give to the residents. Ask the facility what other service projects your group could perform while there, such as weeding the garden, serving lunch, painting, etc. Many hands make light work!

July 12 — Paper Bag Day

+ Use "The Paper Bag Princess" book as your theme and decorate with castles, dragons, princes, and princesses. Have everyone fill a brown lunch sack with an inexpensive gift and decorate the outside. Place all of the bags on the table and everyone who brought a bag gets to pick one out to take home. Serve a sack lunch.

+ Have "Unknown Comedian Night" where people can put a brown bag over their head and tell jokes "anonymously." Fill lunch bags with a little bit of sand and a tea candle to create luminaries outside the entrance walkway. Set out a table with yarn, buttons, glitter, glue, foam shapes, markers, and other craft materials so kids can make brown bag puppets and then put on a show for everyone. Divide into groups and have teams design an outfit made out of paper bags and tape for one of their teammates to wear in a fashion contest.

July 17 — Disneyland opened in 1955.

+ Decorate with all things Disney. Let your imagination run wild!

July 20 — Chess Day

+ Hold a chess tournament for various age brackets. Include checkers for younger children to play. Decorate with white and black décor. Have the children design chess pieces out of play dough or clay. Set out a bunch of chess tables all around the room. You could also create some kind of costume for people to wear depending on what chess piece they want to be and then play a human-sized chess game as a ward. Have children make checkerboard mosaics out of colored tile pieces or strips of colored construction paper. You could decorate with an Alice in Wonderland or Harry Potter theme, focusing on the chess scenes in the stories.

July 24 — Pioneer Day

+ Plan a Pioneer Picnic. This should definitely be a tradition for your ward and there are so many fun activities you can include to honor our pioneer heritage as members of the Church. Some to consider are:
    + Set out quilts on frames so people can work on one while they visit.
    + Have kids look for wrapped candy in piles of hay.
    + Hold potato sack races.
    + Kids make butter by shaking cream in baby food jars while listening to pioneer stories.
    + Play pioneer trivia games or Mormon Jeopardy.
    + Have members write their pioneer ancestors on a giant poster shaped like a wagon. You might even find a few ward members who are related to one another!
    + Sing pioneer songs.
    + Have people dressed as pioneers share inspiring stories.
    + Cook pioneer biscuits over a fire by wrapping dough around a wood block that is attached to a medal rod or stick.
    + Have a Dutch Oven cooking contest.
    + Encourage members to dress as pioneers or set up an area where people can sew pioneer bonnets.
    + Attach those plastic surgical gloves to a cardboard cow over a sawhorse and fill with water so people can try to "milk" the cow.
    + Build handcarts or wagons out of giant appliance boxes.

July 27 — Bugs Bunny's birthday

+ It's all about bunny rabbits, Elmer Fudd, and the Looney Tunes characters. Have an Elmer Fudd contest for the men. To get inspiration and ideas go to www.looneytunes.warnerbros.com

July 30 — National Cheesecake Day

+ Mmmm. Any excuse to eat cheesecake works for me!

CHAPTER 9

August

"August creates as she slumbers,
replete and satisfied."

———————————

JOSEPH WOOD KRUTCH

AUGUST IS...

Science and Technology Month

* Have you ever seen those "Robot Wars" competitions on TV? You could hold a contest where people bring a robot or device to compete against others or else you could provide the parts once they get to the activity and have them assemble them there.

* Hold a good old-fashioned science fair where people can bring their scientific experiments to share with one another. You could also set up stations around the room where people could try out various scientific activities. Have people create their own refreshments by mixing ingredients together to make smoothies, ice cream sundaes, or English trifle. Decorate with microscopes, lab coats, plastic beakers, vials, cylinders, etc.

American Artist Appreciation Month

* Hold a "Meet The Masters" event. Give everyone plenty of time in advance, because you'll be announcing an art contest for all ages. Gather everyone's artwork ahead of time so you'll be able

to display everything on easels and those Cultural Hall dividers. Include artwork from LDS artists, as well as some of the world's famous masterpieces. Have face painting and see if you can borrow one of those Spin-Art machines. Set out pictures of famous art pieces and see if everyone can guess who the artist was. You could probably borrow big copies of famous artwork from your local schools. Some other fun side activities could be:

+ Provide chalk for the children to enjoy sidewalk art. Make sure there are responsible adults to supervise the kids while they're outside!
+ Make Plaster of Paris molds of your guests' hands to take home.
+ Decorate T-shirts with fabric paint.
+ Have everyone decorate their own cookies or cupcakes.
+ Decorate the room to look like a museum with a few benches. See if a local art store would donate free art supplies or gift certificates to award to your "Best of Show" entry or winners in categories such as pencil, acrylic, oils, sculpture, charcoal, scratch board, crayon, crafting materials, quilts, etc.

Foot Health Month

+ Do a Pioneer Trek and call it "Faith In Every Footstep." Invite someone to share a message entitled "STAND as a witness" or "S.T.A.N.D. (Stay True And Never Doubt).
+ Play football and have a Tailgate party. Teach people how to give foot massages and learn about reflexology. Have someone share a message about "Lengthen Your Stride."

Golf Month

+ Host a ward golf tournament. Contact a local golf course and find out what their procedures are. Because of the high expense, all participants will need to pay their own entry fees. Consider creating your very own miniature golf course and tournament at a local park so that everyone can play!

Inventors Month

+ What a great excuse to hold an inventor's contest! People could bring their crazy inventions from home or else you could set out all kinds of random objects which small groups or individuals have to create something out of. Decorate with light bulbs and pictures of Einstein.

Water Quality Month

+ To me, that means Splash Day, a great excuse to include all things water. See if your ward could rent a community pool for a couple of hours or convince a family with a pool to host the event at their house. You can always go outside your building or to a nearby park where you can set up different water stations such as:

WATER BALLOON SQUAT — Each team sends a member to pick up a water balloon who carries it to the finish line and sits on it until it pops. If the balloon pops before they reach the finish line they have to run back to the beginning and get another. The first team who finishes wins.

WATER BALLOON LIMBO — Turn on a water hose and squirt the water out in one thick jet. Limbo contestants have to go under the water without getting wet. After players have successfully gone under once, lower the hose a few inches. The person who is the least wet in the end wins.

WATER BALLOON VOLLEYBALL — Set up a volleyball net or just string a clothesline between two trees. Each team uses a towel or sheet to toss the balloon to the other side. Have plenty of water balloons on hand.

SPONGE BASEBALL — Use the same rules as baseball but use a sponge instead of a ball and kiddie pools filled with water at each base.

WET SPONGE RELAY — Teams dip a huge sponge in a bucket, run to another location where they have to squeeze the water into a bucket and then run back so the next person in line has a turn. The bucket with the most water wins.

OVER & UNDER RELAY — Each team has to pass a wet sponge OVER the head and then UNDER (between the legs), over and under until the last person in line squeezes whatever water is left in the sponge into a bucket. The team with the most water in their container wins.

1st Week of August — Clown Week

• What a perfect time to throw an "Under the Big Top" activity! Drape sheets or inexpensive fabric at the entrances and on the ceiling to give the feel of being inside a circus tent. Hang signs that say "The Greatest Show on Earth" and recruit various people to walk around as circus performers, such as someone on stilts or a juggler. You could set up "rings" with different activities going on in various parts of the Cultural Hall, like games, relays, performances, magic tricks, etc. Invite people to bring their trikes and wagons for a parade with stuffed animals and clowns. Have face painting and a clown contest. Rent one of those popcorn machines and serve peanuts in red and white striped bags. Another twist on a circus event is to serve the meal in courses with circus acts in between. People sitting at each table form a team that has to send someone up on the stage to compete in circus games. Put hula hoops on the stage to represent each table's ring. Contestants would have to juggle, throw soft darts while blindfolded to pop balloons, walk on stilts, toss a bean bag into a clown's mouth cut out of cardboard, balance objects on their head and hands, ride a unicycle, etc.

First Sunday in August — American Family Day

• Celebrate the family by hosting a Family Feud game show activity or a combination of several TV game shows. You could have one big contest that everyone watches or else divide into smaller groups so more people can play. Get some outgoing people to be game-show hosts. You could use a 1960s theme for décor and focus on the game shows that were especially popular then. You can find tons of questions and answers for Family Feud at www. theideadoor.com

- For a more spiritual activity, design "Building A Celestial Family" night with several activities families can do together, such as having their pictures taken all dressed in white, making Family Home Evening packets with ideas and visual aids for future lessons, and participating in silly contests like building a human pyramid or competing against other families in scripture trivia. Decorate with white, angels, clouds and serve angel food cake, divinity, white chocolate desserts and sparkling cider.

- Work with your ward Family History Consultant to host a Family History Fair for the entire community. Decorate with trees (family trees) or gardening décor (digging for your family's roots). Have several tables or displays for fun family history projects such as:
  - How To Plan A Family Reunion
  - Creating A Family Cookbook
  - How To Write Autobiographies and Personal Histories
  - Tips on Interviewing Relatives and Writing Their Biographies
  - Make A Photo Family Tree
  - Hands-On Experience With The Family History Center
  - Using The Internet To Discover Your Roots And Make Connections
  - Using Memorabilia In Crafts
  - Getting Kids Interested In Their Ancestors
  - Honoring Heritage
  - Creating A Lasting Legacy
  - Scrapbooking

- Teach ward members how to throw a family reunion. Set up stations around the room where people could taste good potluck recipes, see samples of clever invitations, play games that work well at reunions, bring photos to scrapbook and display, etc.

- Host a "Family Olympics." Offer a good mix of competitive games so people of all ages and abilities will have a chance of winning something. Throw a twist on categories; for example, the Broad Jump could really be where everyone's height in the family is measured and the team with the biggest number wins. Cross Country Skiing could be where you take a long plank of wood (8-10 ft.)and put straps across it for 5 people or so to stand on it like skis and they have to work together to race another team down and around an obstacle and back to the starting line. Families could decorate potatoes and then have them race (roll) them down a hill. You might also do a race where you have two people run to a designated spot, and then one of them lays down on his back and the other person stands on a chair, dropping spoonfuls of pudding into the other person's mouth. The team which gets the most pudding in the mouth wins.

August 1 — Sports Day

+ Create a field day with games and décor from all kinds of sports. Encourage everyone to wear football jerseys, baseball uniforms or other sport attire. Include some entertainment during your "half time" and serve refreshments at a "concession stand." You could have races for all ages, an obstacle course, jumping rope or hula hoop contest. Invite your local high school cheerleaders to come and teach cheers to the young girls. Have someone share a short message about "Catching The Spirit" or "Go The Distance" to live the gospel faithfully.

+ Hold a Summer Olympics, offering contests in all kinds of sports and games. Construct big Olympic rings out of hula hoops or painted cardboard. Kids could build torches out of colored construction paper. Have a parade of athletes with families dressing alike. Families could also create their own flags. You could spotlight the country that will host the next Olympics. Include competitions that involve brain power, like an Olympic trivia game, so non-athletes can win some events too. Award winners with medals and create a special three-level stage for them to stand on.

August 2 — Ice Cream Sandwich Day

+ Have all kinds of different sandwiches at an indoor or outdoor picnic and ice cream sandwiches, of course, for dessert. Decorate with red and white gingham and plastic ants. This could also just be an ice cream dessert social with some musical entertainment and games.

August 3 — Watermelon Day

+ Would you believe there is an entire web site dedicated to watermelons? It's www.watermelon.org where you'll find trivia, recipes and fun activity ideas just for kids! Have a watermelon carving contest, seed spitting contest, and crafts. This would be a great theme for a ward picnic or outdoor BBQ.

August 5 — Astronaut Neil Armstrong's Birthday (1930)

+ Hold a Space Derby! Get ideas from Cub Scout leaders who may have done one of these events. Allow everyone to enter various categories by age rank. The theme can be "serious" with a focus on astronomy and space exploration or can be geared towards the science fiction fan with aliens and characters from popular science fiction books and movies. Decorate with rocket ships, funny alien drawings, photos of real astronauts or space ships (from NASA web site), drawings or mobiles of the solar system made out of foam. Cover the ceiling with dark blue paper and hang those white Christmas tree lights as stars. Cover cardboard stars with foil or spray paint. You could also put up black lights and use a lot of glow-in-the-dark stars and other décor. Paint rocks in neon or glow-in-the-dark paint. Have an astronaut tell people how much they would weigh on different planets and have a space walk obstacle course or treasure hunt. Play space trivia games and "Pin The Antenna On The Alien." Children could make aliens out of pipecleaners, pompoms, modeling clay and wiggle eyes. Make and decorate space ships out of large boxes.

August 15 — Relaxation Day

+ Here's an event that's so easy to plan that even your committee will feel relaxed! Have a "Low Country Boil." Tape rolls of white butcher paper to long tables and set out a few buckets and paper towels. No plates, no utensils. Low country boil consists of cooking potatoes, shrimp, corn on the cob, sausage, green beans, crab seasoning and onions all in one pot. Drain the water and dump contents along the table where people pick and choose the pieces they want to eat with their fingers. Play Cajon music and throw in some ice breaker games and you'll have an extremely relaxing, casual party with some southern charm. Clean-up is a snap because you only have to roll up the butcher paper and throw it away.

+ Create an all-inclusive resort feeling by setting out stations where people can participate in various activities at their leisure. Decorate with a tropical motif, serving fruity drinks and Smoothies with umbrellas in them. Set out croquet, create a shuffleboard court area with real or play equipment, display food on a banquet table with fancy table linens and props, design a "spa" where guests can get a pedicure or massage, and recruit the help of the youth to dress up as waiters who wander around offering appetizers or drinks on trays.

August 22 — Be An Angel Day

+ Entitle your event "Angels Among Us", "The Errand Of Angels" or "Hands of Heaven" and decorate with lots and lots of angels! Have a service auction. Everyone has to donate an item or service that can be auctioned off. When everyone arrives they will be given a list of all the items they can bid on. They earn bidding dollars or points by answering a questionnaire that awards them a certain amount of points for things they have done that day or week such as praying, reading the scriptures, hugging a parent, attending Seminary, doing homework, going Home Teaching, changing a diaper, etc. It's quite entertaining to see the competitive spirit emerge from members who are bidding for the same item! Decorate with lots of angels, clouds hanging from the ceiling, and halos. You'll find tons of angel crafts to keep the kids busy at www.craftycollege.com/webofangels/

August 30 — Toasted Marshmallow Day

+ Call your activity "In The Line Of Fire." It probably won't be hard to find some men in your ward who want to show off their BBQ skills. Show people how to grill different kinds of meat, chicken, fish, veggies, fruit and bread. People could make and decorate BBQ aprons or have a dutch oven cooking contest. Use those cute marshmallow S'more ornaments as your inspiration piece for decorations. Children could even make their own little S'more people out of graham crackers, chocolate, marshmallows and other candies to accessorize with hats, hands, faces, etc. This would need to be an outdoor activity or campout. Set up fires or BBQ pits made out of foil lined, heavy cardboard boxes. Teach the children how to wrap dough strips on a stick and toast over coals.

CHAPTER 10

September

"September: it was the most beautiful of words, he'd always felt, evoking orange-flowers, swallows, and regret."

ALEXANDER THEROUX

SEPTEMBER IS...

School Success Month

+ Using a "Back To School" theme, decorate with apples, school busses, lunch boxes, globes, maps, pencils, backpacks, rulers, desks, etc. You might even convince a teacher or school to let you borrow a few items. Play "Are You Smarter Than A 5th Grader?" with the Primary children and adults who are willing to embarrass themselves! Serve refreshments cafeteria-style complete with food trays and ladies in hair nets serving up the grub. You could also serve refreshments in brown lunch bags or showcase creative lunch ideas. Design your invitations to look like report cards or homework ("Your first assignment is to attend this party and have a great time.") Play Dodgeball, Simon Says, or "Kickin It Old School" relays where people have to pack a lunch box, sip an entire juice box, put papers in a binder, erase a chalkboard, fly a paper airplane, run with a backpack and other school tasks. Set out a word search for school movies like *Ferris*

Bueller's Day Off, Never Been Kissed, or *The Dead Poet's Society.* You could even schedule the party like a school day and ring a bell between the following sessions: home room (arriving), PE (games and activities), Art (arts and crafts), recess (free play), and lunch time (refreshments).

+ Decorate with a college motif and entitle your activity "Eternity University." Have people go to "classes" where they participate in games, crafts and eat food like angel food cake.

National Childhood Cancer Awareness Month

+ Visit www.canceradvocacy.org to learn more about what kinds of service projects your ward could do to help.

+ As a ward, throw a party for children in your area who are cancer patients. Call your local children's hospital to find out more what you can do.

Baby Safety Month

+ Throw a baby shower for your building's nursery by encouraging everyone to bring a new or gently used toy to donate to the nursery. Clean the nursery and play silly baby shower games. You'll find tons of ideas (101 to be exact) at www.101babyshowerideas. com

Breakfast Month

+ Have a breakfast potluck or cooking contest so people can showcase their soufflés, crepes, eggs Benedict, coffee-cakes, and other breakfast recipes.

Children's Health and Safety Month

+ Have fun with a medical theme and emphasize how the gosPILL keeps us spiritually healthy. Set up a pharmacist area where you serve candy in prescription bottles. Decorate with medical supplies. Wear white medical coats, surgies, or those surgical coats. Invite someone to give a short message on how Christ is the "Master Healer" and the "Great Physician."

Classical Music Month

+ Introduce your ward to the finer side of music, by hosting an elegant event that features some of the classical composers and their music. Set up tables or booths that share information on the culture and country of several composers with food, décor, and photos. Encourage musicians in your ward to perform some pieces as well.

Chicken Month

+ Using a chicken theme, have a good old-fashioned country-western hoe-down! Teach the ward how to do country line dancing or square dancing. Paint cows on white cardboard taped to sawhorses and attach some water-filled hospital gloves below so people can try to "milk" the cows for some "udder" nonsense. You might be able to convince a local clogging or square dance group to perform for your ward. Pan for gold by spray painting gold onto rocks and burying them in a sand-filled container. Be sure to put a tarp down underneath, do it outside, or use rice instead of sand for easier clean-up. Set out a quilt in a corner for those who would rather tie quilts or sew than dance. Have a hog-calling contest and award the winner with a pound of bacon. Decorate with lots of cowboy hats, boots, bandanas and encourage guests to come dressed in western attire. Put a cardboard horse head on a bale of hale for the kids to try and rope. Go to www.country-time.com for some ideas on music, dances, and links to other line dancing web sites. Create a "jail" where "sheriffs" kidnap misbehaving party guests. In order for people to get their criminal friend out of jail they have to sing Primary songs on a microphone for all to hear. Use some rubber chickens as décor or as part of a game where you toss them into a pot from a distance.

+ Focusing on chickens, hold a "Country Fair" where each auxiliary is asked to provide one activity booth. Have a blue ribbon cooking contest for dessert entries or jams, face painting, balloon animals, and try to rent one of those cotton candy machines. Encourage ward members to bring craft items they have made at home to display. Invite the bishop or an outgoing host to dress up like Old MacDonald and reenact the song with ward members. Serve hot dogs or fried chicken, corn on the cob, biscuits, watermelon, pickles on a stick, root beer and lots of pie.

Courtesy Month

+ Have an etiquette dinner where everyone can practice their good manners. Invite several families who are willing to host tables and bring their nice dishes from home and who could decorate their table very formally. Try to recruit the Elders Quorum or youth to serve as waiters who can serve tables, dressed in their suits with a towel over their arm like in nice restaurants. Invite married couples to act out good dates and bad dates as funny skits. Play the Newlywed game. Teach ward members how to ballroom dance. You could also decorate with a "My Fair Lady" theme and get ward members to perform the various songs from the famous musical.

+ Throw a "Tacky Time" party where everyone is encouraged to dress tacky. Everyone brings their own dinner (because that's tacky) or else have a cooking with Spam contest. Serve "Dirt Cake" for dessert. Ask several families to decorate one table each and let them know you'll be awarding a prize for the most tacky décor. Find out who is the most tacky person worthy of a prize by playing this entertaining game that was a hit in a ward: Everyone starts standing up and then the MC says something like "If you've never wrapped up a gift you've received but didn't like and then given it to someone else, sit down...If you've never gone through the express lane at the grocery store with more than the allowed number of items, sit down...If you've never paid your taxes ON April 15th, sit down...etc. The last one standing is the "tackiest".

Recruit the help of the youth to put on a tacky fashion show. Have an MC announce the model and point out the tacky fashion problem such as a RISING HEM LINE (helium balloons attached to the skirt), TURTLE NECK (pictures of turtles on the neck), and SMOKING JACKET (dry ice in the pocket of a jacket). You can also have a talent show, encouraging people to really ham up their act. The funnier, the better.

Honey Month

+ Using President Gordon B. Hinckley's "To Be" theme, decorate with honeybees and hives and emphasize all of the good things we ought to "bee." It could be a dessert only event or a dinner with food that includes honey in the recipe, such as honey-baked ham, biscuits and honey, etc.

Piano Month

+ What a great excuse for a talent show! You could include all talents or emphasize only musical ones to go with the theme of pianos. Decorate everything in black and white and musical notes. A simple but elegant decoration is to fill a white box with fluffed-up black tissue paper, set a musical instrument inside and have white musical notes and sheet music spilling out. Introduce ward members to Mormon musicians by spotlighting some of their songs. You could also use "American Idol" as your theme. Invite members to perform and give everyone a participation award. You could also give silly awards such as "Most Likely to appear on the David Letterman Show" or "Most likely to be recruited by the Mormon Tabernacle Choir".

+ Host a piano recital for everyone in the ward who is taking piano lessons or has in the past. Have families make a musical aid for their Family Home Evenings. One example is to create an elephant face out of cardstock and then use a sock to look like the elephant trunk. The child puts his hand in the trunk and moves it around to follow a 2/4, 4/4 or 6/8 music pattern. Play "Name That Tune" using Primary songs or hymns. Have someone share a short message about being in TUNE with the Spirit or how going to church to worship together is like playing all of the keys on a piano rather than staying home and trying to play a song with only one note by one's self.

Rice Month

+ Use a Chinese motif with ideas from February's Chinese New Year ideas.

First Monday in September — Labor Day

+ Honor the day of hard work by setting up an assembly line to build racks and rotating shelves for food storage for families who would like one.

+ Have a ward picnic potluck. Emphasize the "key" to success is hard work by setting out a craft table where people can make hangers to hold their keys.

+ Let ward members share the "fruit of their labors" during the summer by showcasing their homemade jams, jellies and other foods they have canned at a ward breakfast. A fun Taster's Table would be filled with different kinds of rolls, muffins, toast, and bread to sample all the flavors of jellies and jams. Serve other kinds of jams like jalepeno jelly over cream cheese served with crackers, or mint jelly that compliments roast lamb. Decorate jars with home-made labels and cute lids with fabric covers.

+ Have a country fair where people can showcase their handicrafts and projects they have been laboring on. Award blue ribbons, have entertainment, decorate with lots of gingham fabric and raffia, and allow everyone to sample homemade jams, syrups, vinegars, pies, etc.

First Sunday After Labor Day — National Grandparents Day

+ As a ward, visit a local nursing home to perform songs, bring cards the Primary children have made, paint the old ladies' nails, and talk to the residents. Check with the facility to see if you could even bring some pets for the residents to play with. You'll find some great ideas for activities and crafts at www. grandparents-day.com/activities.htm

+ Prepare a special dinner for the older people in your ward.

+ Have a "Then and Now" party where people can invite their

grandparents to attend. Compare things that were popular back then with now, such as "American Bandstand" vs. American Idol.

+ Plan a picnic where families can bring their older relatives to enjoy the outdoors together. Arrange for someone in your ward to serve as a photographer who will take group family photos.

3rd Tuesday in September — International Day of Peace

+ The day is devoted to commemorating and strengthening the ideals of peace both within and among all nations and peoples. Invite other religions to join you in a day of music or fun outdoor games.

+ Organize a cultural fair for your community. To see what other groups have done, go to www.peaceoneday.org

First Saturday after Labor Day — Public Lands Day

+ Keep America Beautiful Foundation has tons of service project ideas for your ward to help beautify your local parks, beaches, roads and public buildings. They even offer a "Home Town USA" award to Boy Scouts who perform service projects that protect the environment. You can also check out Take Pride in America. You're probably familiar with Adopt-A-Highway, but did you know your ward could also adopt a waterway? For more information go to www.adoptahighway.com and www.adoptawaterway.com or write to:

Keep America Beautiful, Inc.
Mill River Plaza
9 W. Broad Street
Stamford, CT 0690

September 6 — Read a Book Day

+ Host a Book Night where kids and their families create and bind their own book. You might be able to borrow one of those spiral binding machines from a local school for the night. Invite local authors to speak and set up cozy corners where children can sit and read or have a Bishopric member read to them. Help ward members become more familiar with LDS authors by spotlighting several books in fiction and non-fiction. Even better, invite an LDS author to speak to your ward about literacy, writing or their own books! You could also invite someone to speak on "Don't Judge A Book By Its Cover" and celebrate all of the different personalities in your ward. Check out www.ldsstorymakers.com to find an author near you. You can also email them a request for a speaker at Literacy@ldstorymakers.com Many of them have special literacy presentations they would gladly share with your group.

- Focus on the very best books: the scriptures! Entitle your event "Feast Upon the Words of Christ." Create stations in different rooms of your building where everyone could participate in different activities. Have a "Taster's Table" of foods from the Bible such as dates, figs, olives, barley, etc. Play a Who's Who game for party guests to test their Bible trivia. You could also have a "Smell Session" where ward members could smell common Bible fragrances such as frankincense, myrrh, cardamom, coriander, hyssop, etc. Make bookmarks for the scriptures and showcase different ways of marking scripture passages with colored pencils, stickers, codes, etc. Mark key scriptures in copies of the Book of Mormon for the missionaries to pass out to their investigators. Have families dress up in Bible-time tunics and robes to take pictures. Design games that could be played on Sundays or during Family Home Evening that test scripture skills such as games from the *Friend* magazine or a Seminary Scripture Chase. Use your Seminary and Gospel Doctrine teachers as a resource for other games and activities. For dessert that evening you could have an "Articles of Faith Bar" where each Article of Faith represents a different item such as a spoon, bowl, napkin, ice cream scoop, and different toppings. When members recite an Article of Faith they receive each of the corresponding items. Make bookmarks for the scriptures and showcase different ways of marking scripture passages.

September 12 — Chocolate Milkshake Day

+ Decorate the Cultural Hall to look like an old-fashioned malt shoppe, using small tables and chairs, 50's décor, and ice cream sundaes and malts made out of painted Styrofoam balls. It could be a 1950s Sock Hop or just an activity with lots of 1950s music playing and a DJ. Put a Harley Davidson motorcycle in a corner with a photographer to take pictures of the kids posing on it. Fill tall soda fountain glasses with mint and pink tissue paper sticking out for table decorations. Scatter Bubble Gum on the tables for the kids to take. Serve root beer floats or cream sodas. Make a life-size stand-up poster of James Dean, and other 50's celebrities.

+ Decorate with a cow motif and serve lots of different kinds of ice cream, shakes, smoothies and sorbets.

+ Celebrate chocolate by hosting a dessert social and decorating with browns, pink and white décor. See the "Death by Chocolate" idea listed under May 15.

September 13 — Author Roald Dahl's Birthday, 1916

+ Check out www.roalddahl.com to learn more about the author of the famous "Charlie and the Chocolate Factory", "James and the Giant Peach" and other fun books. Decorate with a "Charlie and the Chocolate Factory" theme and invite people to the event with a golden ticket. Have a Scrumdidilyumptious Dessert Contest and invite the missionaries or Bishopric to judge. Hold an Augustus Gloop chocolate pudding eating contest, Violet Beauregarde Bubble Blowing Contest, Veruca Salt Golden Egg relay, Mike Teavee's LDS movie trivia, and an Oompa Loompa dance off. Award winners with Wonka candy.

September 13 — Scooby-Doo's Birthday

+ Throw a murder mystery dinner! Decorate in 1970s style and include all the goofy goblins, ghosts and characters from the fun Scooby-Doo cartoons and movies. For inspiration go to www.cartoonnetwork.com/tv_shows/scooby/index.html Have a little haunted trail, a mystery to solve and lots of Scooby snacks throughout the evening. Have a contest to see who can look and sound the most like the characters on the show.

September 13 — Peanut Day

+ Use a peanut farmer theme and invite everyone to learn how to make peanut butter by grinding their own peanuts. Kids could make little characters and scenes out of peanuts in their shell. Serve BBQ. Have someone dress up like Jimmy Carter to "visit" the party. Introduce ward members to the southern traditional dish of boiled peanuts. Use those cornstarch-based packing peanuts to have a sculpture-making contest. (Wet the ends with your tongue and the peanuts will stick together.)

September 17 — Apple Dumpling Day

+ "Apples" is a perfect theme for a party in September because people are also thinking about going back to school and bringing that classic apple to put on their teacher's desk. Have an apple festival and invite everyone to enter an apple cooking contest. All entries have to use apples in the recipe. Have apple dunking and core tossing contests. You could use a real country fair theme with blue ribbons and lots of gingham fabric and raffia. Invite the Primary to sing and call them the "Apple Dumpling Gang." Fill mason jars with dried apple chips to set out on tables for people to snack on.

September 17 — Constitution Day

+ Dress several people in costume to resemble some of the famous signers of the Declaration of Independence and invite them to share short messages about the founding of the country.

September 18 — Mushroom Picking Day

+ Have a "Farmer's Market" where people can swap all of the fruits and veggies they've grown during the summer. Award blue ribbons for the best produce. Serve a salad bar.

+ Have a fairytale-themed event featuring toadstools. Make giant mushrooms by covering padded cardboard circles with fabric and placing them on thick cardboard tubes.

September 21 — Mini Golf Day

+ Create a Mormon miniature golf course in the cultural hall or even going down the hallways in the building, using various supplies from your local hardware store, giant cardboard boxes from appliances, and miscellaneous items such as sleds, rain gutters, food storage cans, tables, chairs, and sports equipment. You could also divide into groups and have each group create their own hole to add to the whole course. Ask your local miniature golf center to let you borrow some of their putters to use. A golf store may even have some damaged ones they'll let you use. Provide a short lesson on how to hold a golf club correctly, a gentle reminder about treating the building with respect, scorecards, a trophy for the winning team, and then let the game begin! Decorate a cake with green frosting to look like grass and with a small dab of frosting attach a donut hole to a golf tee to put in several places on the cake. Have someone give a short talk about how to stay "on the ball" in the Church.

September 23 — Autumn Begins

+ Celebrate the arrival of autumn with a traditional Fall Festival! Have a scarecrow-making contest, do leaf rubbings, decorate with gourds, make birdhouses, and play games. See more ideas listed under October 31.

CHAPTER 11

October

"O hushed October morning mild,
Begin the hours of this day slow.
Make the day seem to us less brief."

ROBERT FROST
"October"

OCTOBER IS...

Apple Month

+ Pick apples together at a nearby apple farm and have an outdoor picnic.

Computer Learning Month

+ Recruit the help of your Ward Employment Specialist to offer classes and activities that teach people how to improve their computer skills.

Dessert Month

+ Hold a dessert baking contest.
+ Set up several stations where people taste things and participate in activities such as:

"Sweet Is The Work" – Ward members write letters to the missionaries.

"Pie In Your Face" – Throw whipped cream pies at volunteers whose faces are sticking out of holes cut out of a plastic tarp. The bishopric always make popular victims.

"Have Your Cake And Eat It Too" – Have a cupcake decorating contest. Teach people how to make frosting roses.

"That's The Way The Cookie Crumbles" – Decorate cookies. Toss fake cookies into baskets to win prizes.

"I Scream, You Scream, We All Scream For Ice Cream" – People make sculptures out of ice cream. Everyone earns a scoop, bowl, spoon, and various toppings for each Article of Faith they can recite.

"Chocoholics Anonymous" – People dip fruit, cake, cream puffs, pretzels, etc in a chocolate fountain. Everyone could make chocolate covered spoons to wrap and give as a gift.

"Candy Land" – Create a large version of this popular game for groups to play.

Roller Skating Month

+ Go roller skating as a ward at a local roller rink and see if you can get a group discount or rent the whole place for a couple of hours. If the cost is prohibitive, create your own roller rink by using the church parking lot or another safe area. You could have a 1950s theme and serve hamburgers in the cars, using the Young Women to bring food like roller waitresses.

Second Monday in October — Columbus Day

+ With the help of your ward Cub Scout leaders, plan a Rain Gutter Regatta. Purchase sailboat kits at your local scout store or online $3.99 each at www.scoutstuff.org Even cheaper than that (free) is to get a school cafeteria to let you have their empty milk cartons after lunch. Clean them with bleach and dry before passing them out at the party. Members add a straw and a sail made out of paper. Pass out kits a week or so before the event so families have time to prepare and decorate them or else set up tables and allow time during the party. If that price is too expensive, just have people bring whatever craft they want to that fits inside the rain gutter and award prizes for "Most Unusual Watercraft", "Most Likely To Capsize", "Coolest Design", etc. Fill special gutters with water and have racers blow the sails on their boats to the finish line. For decorations for the room, build ships out of big cardboard appliance boxes, muslin fabric, and ropes. Create one of those standing cardboard figures to look like Christopher Columbus so people can put their faces in the hole and take funny pictures next to the ship. Invite someone to read the account of Christopher Columbus in 1 Nephi 13 and read accounts of how he was led by the spirit to arrive in the Americas.

2nd Week of October — Fire Prevention Week

+ Invite your local Fire Department to give demonstrations and be a resource for you. They usually have free firemen hats they can give to the children, literature for parents, and sometimes even free crafts for the kids like making a fire engine out of construction paper. Provide grid paper so families can draw the floor plan of their house and design an escape plan. Many Fire Departments also have a cool "Smoke House" they can bring that ward members could crawl through to learn what it feels like to escape from a house that's on fire. Have a "3 Alarm Chili Cook-off" or a "Smokin BBQ." Set up a display table with items that should be in a 72 hour bag or Emergency Preparedness Kit. Have a "Bucket Brigade" relay where teams scoop water from a tub with a bucket and race a short distance where they dump their water into another tub. The team with the most water in their tub at the end wins. Divide party guests into teams, lining people up in front of one another to have a Firemen's Hat Relay. Hand the first person in each line a firemen's hat who has to pass it under his legs. The next person in line has to pass it over his head. Keep alternating until the last person reverses it and passes it back to the first person in line. The first team to finish wins. Have Smokey the Bear make an appearance. Check out www.smokeybear.com for other ideas.

October 2 — Peanuts Comic Strip First Published in 1950

* Get inspiration from all the Charles Shulz Peanuts characters at www.snoopy.com Charlie Brown and the Great Pumpkin could make for a really cute theme for your annual Halloween party!

October 12 — Farmer's Day

* Have a Harvest Festival, complete with hay rides, leaf rubbings, and a hoe down. Make bookmarks with leaf stamps.
* Have a fancy Harvest Ball with elegant autumn décor.

October 16 — World Food Day

* Help distribute boxes of food at a food bank, start a food drive, or serve food at a local soup kitchen. To learn more about what your ward can do, write to:

World Food Day
National Coordinator
National Committee for World Food Day
1001 22nd Street NW
Washington, DC 20437

* Reserve a night at your local Family Home Storage Center where families will learn how to can food in Mylar sealed pouches or #10 size cans. Set out a table where everyone can taste samples.
* Plan an international feast, with booths set up to represent different countries. Recruit the help of your ward's returned missionaries to host a table for their country. Showcase music, food, dances, and decorations from around the world. Hang international flags around the room or posters painted to look like them. In the center of the room paint a big earth on round poster paper or create a big one out of Styrofoam to display. Hang a map of the world and have people put stickers or push pins where they have traveled. Invite someone to share a message about how the gospel is spreading all over the world.

- Hold a "Taste of Alpharetta" activity, using the name of your town and recruiting help from local restaurants. This could be a fun community outreach event. Invite restaurants and other food venues in your area to provide small samples of their most popular dishes for guests to taste. Set up booths around the room with some entertainment to keep the evening moving. Decorate with chef hats, aprons, kitchen utensils, menus, and waiters.

October 24 — United Nations Day

- Hold an Oktoberfest, highlighting German food, dancing, polka, music, and of course apple strudel! Skip the beer and focus on the lederhosen. Find out which ward members can trace their heritage to Germany. The official colors of the German state of Bavaria (home to the Oktoberfest) are cobalt blue and snow white. Suspend a basket of flowers from the middle of the ceiling and hang streamers, radiating out to the ceiling edges. Use mugs as vases for flowers, utensil holders or for snacks on tables. Adorn walls with posters of Germany, and flags from the 16 German states. Kids could decorate paper aprons and suspenders to wear. Get ward members to create an oompah band and give party guests kazoos to play along. Include some group dancing and a few songs from the musical "The Sound of Music." Introduce ward members to the flavors of German sausages, hot German potato salad, sauerkraut, sweet and sour cabbage, German-style chicken, and Black Forest cake.

October 31 — Halloween

The Halloween tradition has become a bit controversial in our country with many Christians in past years. Talk with your bishop for help in deciding the tone of this party. Remember, the goals of every activity should be to bring souls to Christ and to fellowship both Church members and non-members. Below is a list of party possibilities that range from ones that attempt to veer away from the ghoulish customs of Halloween and focus more on fall festival items to the traditional pumpkin carnival with costumes, spook alley and creepies.

- There is a very cute idea for a Halloween Carnival with a Book of Mormon theme on www.theideadoor.com
- Spotlight scarecrows and decorate with a Wizard of Oz theme, using ideas from April 3.
- Items to include during a traditional Halloween carnival:
  - Number the bottom of some small gourds or pumpkins and float them in a tub of water. Children get to choose one and if they pick one that is marked, they win a small prize.
  - Make wooden black cats with a tall stick-like tail to hold donuts. Serve a punch bowl full of green Kool-Aid and Sprite, with a witch hat floating in it (black paper plate with a black party hat glued onto it).
  - Put 10 carved pumpkin faces made out of construction paper on the floor in a circle to have a Cake Walk, Cupcake Walk, or Cookie Walk. Play music and when the music stops the person standing on the specially-marked pumpkin wins a treat.
  - Create an "Apple Picking" board by making a large apple tree with lots of red apples out of construction paper and taping it over a peg board. Poke lollipops through the peg board, marking the bottoms of a few of the lollipop sticks. Kids get to "pick" an apple. Everyone gets to keep the lollipop they choose and marked sticks earn them an additional prize.
  - Hang donuts from strings that people have to try to eat. The person who can finish their donut in 10 seconds wins a box of donuts or some other prize.
  - Float apples in a tub of water for "Apple Bobbing." The first person who can show 3 separate bite holes wins a prize. All players get to keep their apples.
  - Invite the Young Women to offer their face painting skills.
  - Provide an empty Trick or Treat pumpkin so the children can donate some of their candy to a women and children's shelter and feel the joy of service.
  - Encourage members to enter their carved pumpkins in a contest and announce ahead of time that all participants

will receive a prize and winners will receive something even better. Set the entries out in a prominent spot to add a decorative element to the room. Have ward members vote for their favorite by turning in a voting sheet before the end of the night. Another way to judge is to give each guest a special ticket when they enter the party and allow them to put the ticket in the specially-designated ballot box next to the pumpkin they like the best. The box with the most tickets at the end of the night wins.

- Decorate with balloon ghosts (balloons covered with white cloth, netting or garbage bags).
- Make skeletons out of cardboard or white PVC pipes to hang on walls or sit on chairs at each table.
- Hang spider webs made out of yarn stretching across prominent doors and bathroom stalls.
- Toss Hula Hoops over large pumpkins.
- Toss bean bags into the mouth of a painted pumpkin or ghost, using a cardboard box or wood board.
- Play Hot Potato but use a small pumpkin.
- Instead of a Spook Alley, try a "House of Tricks":
    1. Walk the plank: Blind-fold the guest, but hold his hand while he walks up to the plank which is only about 6 inches off the floor. He'll think he's walking very high because the "host" is ducking down lower and lower until he can barely hold on to person's hand. At the end the host says to jump.
    2. Guessing boxes: Place various toys and non-icky items in boxes with holes cut in them and have the guest guess the contents.
    3. Gooshy Box: Place small, plastic toys inside a container full of Jell-O or cooked spaghetti noodles. The guest reaches in, without seeing, and gets to choose an item to keep.
- Find other ideas at www.halloweenmagazine.com

CHAPTER 12

November

"How sad would be November if we had
no knowledge of the spring!

EDWIN WAY TEALE

NOVEMBER IS...

Aviation Month

+ Entitle your event "The Rising Generation" or "Aspire Higher" and decorate with hot air balloons.

+ Create a "Fly United" activity to increase the unity in your ward. Play lots of team-building games and decorate with an airplane motif.

Latin American Month

+ Check out the fun ideas for a Mexican fiesta under May 5.

Fourth Thursday — Thanksgiving (USA)

+ See ideas listed under "Thank You Month" in January. Make "Thankfulness Trees" by twisting brown bags to make them look like a trunk and branches. Have families write what they are thankful for on colorful leaves and glue them to their branches as a take-home gift they can enjoy during the holidays. Kids could make "Thankful chains" by writing things they are grateful for on slips of paper and gluing the loops to form a chain. They could use it as an advent calendar for the Christmas season next month. Set out stationery where people can write thank you notes to each other, to their family members, to the Bishopric or other Church leaders, or to the missionaries and servicemen who are serving away from home. Set out a big roll of butcher paper for people to write what they're thankful for and draw pictures that can be hung in the nursery for a little while. Draw a tree on poster paper for each family (or just one for the ward) and have the children trace around their hands on colored paper to make leaves where they can write their names and their blessings.

+ Hold a "Turkey Trot" marathon in the morning with a breakfast and Thanksgiving festivities afterward. Build a Mayflower out of a big refrigerator box and muslin fabric for sails. Play "Pin The Feather On The Turkey." Make pilgrim hats and Indian headbands for kids to wear.

+ Begin a tradition of an annual "Turkey Bowl" football game. Include a flag football game for the people who don't want full body contact. Serve bowls of turkey soup with a wonderful selection of rolls and bread. Divide people into small groups and give them each a bowl of miscellaneous props they have to include in a skit.

+ Show your gratitude by doing a service project. Prepare bag lunches or dinners to donate to a soup kitchen or a homeless shelter for the holidays. Make an assembly line where ward members fill bags with various food items and non-perishable snacks.

National Family Week

+ Go to www.nationalfamilyweek.org to learn about this week designated for families to serve in their communities.

+ Entitle your event "Sacred Seals" and emphasize that families can be together forever. Invite a young couple who has recently been married in the temple to share some of their experiences about temple marriage. Display pictures of other ward members who were married in temples. Decorate the room by displaying wedding dresses of ward members and their temple photos. Invite a family who has recently been sealed in the temple to talk about that special day. Serve wedding cake and use white décor. Invite your nearest temple presidency to speak about your temple.

◆ Entitle your event "Homespun Happiness" and set up a bunch of stations where families could work on various craft projects together, such as making or decorating frames to display "The Family: A Proclamation To The World." Another station could be a presentation about what the Proclamation means and how we can stand for truth and righteousness in our community. You can also print the Proclamation on vellum and place it over a picture of each family or one of Christ. Set up a nice background where families can get their pictures taken. Share ideas and make packets for Family Home Evening. Play goofy games where families compete together. Set out display tables that help families get ideas for planning a family reunion such as invitations, get-to-know-you games, gifts, banners, matching clothing items, locations, food, entertainment, cost, kids activities, housing, and ideas for video presentations and scrapbooks.

November 3 — Sandwich Day (invented on this day in 1762)

◆ Have a Sub or "Hero" Sandwich Bar where people can build their own sandwiches with lots of different things to choose from: meats, grilled veggies, sauces, cheeses, different breads and rolls, etc. Serve ice cream sandwiches for dessert. Have a brown bag decorating contest. Invite someone to share a short message entitled "The Hero Within."

November 4 — King Tut's Tomb Discovered, 1922

◆ Time for an Egyptian party! Encourage everyone to dress in Egyptian attire and award prizes for the best costumes. Fill the room with palm trees, posters of pyramids, sphinx, hieroglyphics, jewels, and a paper river Nile taped to the floor that goes across the room.

November 4 — Candy Day

+ When everyone walks in they select a candy bar out of a basket filled with 5 different kinds. Later, all of the people who selected a "Snickers" have to tell some jokes. The people who chose another candy bar have to do a skit, dance, song, etc. Another twist is that all of the people who choose the same candy have to sit together for dessert.

November 11 — Veterans Day, commemorates the ending of World War I

+ Borrow patriotic ideas from Memorial Day listed in May. In addition, get the Young Men and Young Women to dance a swing. Have the High Priests and Relief Society sisters sing songs from World War I era. See if you can find a Scottish group in town who could play "Amazing Grace" on the bagpipes. Invite Veterans in your ward to bring medals and photos to display on a table. Prepare care packages that could be sent to soldiers overseas. Visit these websites to find military personnel your ward could adopt:

  Be an Angel to a Soldier: www.soldiersangels.org
  Be a Penpal: www.mysoldier.com
  Adopt a Soldier: www.adoptasoldier.us
  Adopt a Platoon: www.adoptaplatoon.org

November 14 — Clean Out Your Refrigerator Day

+ Sounds like a good excuse to have a potluck. Then again, yuck.

November 15 — America Recycles Day

+ Entitle your event "Another Man's Treasure" and hold a ward junk exchange. Everyone receives a barter ticket for each item they bring. People could "purchase" items as an auction or by paying the assigned price (placed on a sticker by your committee). Have someone teach the ins and outs of having a garage sale, how to prepare, price and display items. You could also host a real garage sale as a fundraiser for the youth's summer camps.

November 26 — Cake Day

- A dessert potluck would be sweet! (Pun intended.) Invite ward members to enter cakes in a baking contest and award winners with prizes. Decorate with a French motif and advertise with the famous words allegedly spoken by Marie Antoinette "Let Them Eat Cake!"

- This could be a fundraiser for the youth to earn money for summer camps where cakes are auctioned off after a potluck dinner.

CHAPTER 13

December

"Every year at just this time,
In cold and dark December,
Families around the world
All gather to remember,
With presents and with parties,
With feasting and with fun,
Customs and traditions
for people old and young."

HELEN H. MOORE

The Christmas season is magical and allows for special activities that unite and create lasting memories like no other time of year. It's also an extremely busy time of year, so remember to be mindful of the hectic schedule your ward members have. Be careful to not overplan during the holidays, but to choose activities that are meaningful and draw your brothers and sisters closer to the Savior and the "reason for the season." Inviting Santa Clause to your Christmas party has been somewhat controversial lately, so talk with your bishop first to see how he feels about it. Another option is to dress the Bishopric as the Three Wise Men and have them pass out small gifts to the children. As always, be mindful of fire code regulations that prohibit the use of candles and real Christmas trees.

DECEMBER IS ...

Hello Neighbor Month

- Help ward members reach out to their neighbors by giving them lots of ideas for inexpensive gifts, homemade goodies and other treats that they could take as holiday gifts. Create work stations where ward members can make crafts or assemble treats on decorative plates.

- Organize a cookie exchange where members who want to participate each bring several dozen cookies to share and trade with others. Plates of cookies can be given to neighbors, enjoyed by the members or used as refreshments for each family to host their own Christmas party.

- One month before the Christmas activity night have ward members pick each other's names out of a hat to determine who will be a "Secret Santa" for whom. During the next few weeks the members can do all kinds of anonymous service or give little gifts. You may want to establish certain guidelines that limit the dollar amount of spending to encourage ward members to be more creative and so it won't be a financial burden. At the Christmas party all of the Secret Santas will reveal themselves to each other. Often times there will be people who go all out while others don't do very much. Be sure that it is a voluntary experience so that only the families who really get excited about this idea will participate, while others who don't want to do it can gracefully slip out.

- "Hey, hey, hay!" Create a hay wagon for outdoor caroling. Drive by peoples' homes while singing Christmas carols.

Safe Toy and Gift Month

- Check out www.toysfortots.org to find out what your ward can do to help gather and donate safe toys for children in need of extra love and attention during the holidays.

- Have a baby shower for your ward nursery, using ideas found under "Baby Safety Month" in September.

Write to a Friend Month

+ Whether you have a casual potluck or a full-blown Christmas extravaganza, be sure to set out stationery, stickers, rubber stamps and envelopes so ward members can send Christmas greetings to the missionaries serving from your ward, as well as military servicemen and women, and college students who are away from home during the holidays.

December 1 — Pie Day

+ Decorate with a Greek motif and label the event "I Eta Pi." Encourage ward members to enter their home baked pies in a contest and award prizes to winners of serious and goofy categories such as "Best Crust", "Most Appealing", "Most Unique", "Best fruit pie", "Tastiest Cream Pie", "Best of Show", "Most Likely To Get You On Martha Stewart's Show As A Guest", etc. Invite someone to share a short message about what P.I.E. might stand for, such as: "Peace In Eternity." Have a pie-eating contest and throw whip cream-filled pie tins at members of the Bishopric who pop their heads out of a decorated tarp. Draw funny characters on the front and be sure to send them home with a nice pie for being good sports.

December 3 — International Day of the Disabled Person

+ Organize a Merit Badge day for the Boy Scouts to earn the Disability Awareness merit badge.

+ Find out how your ward could volunteer at the Special Olympics. Go to www.specialolympics.org

December 3 — Roof-Over-Your-Head Day

+ Invite everyone to build their own gingerbread houses to display in their homes during the holidays. Supply lots of candies, frosting, and gingerbread. An inexpensive and simple way to construct a building is to use graham crackers instead of gingerbread materials. Borrow holiday ideas from some of the suggestions under December to create a more festive party. Have a gingerbread man decorating contest. Make some of them look like missionaries or people from the scriptures or from church history.

December 4 — Cookie Day

◆ Organize a cookie exchange where members who want to participate each bring several dozen cookies to share and trade with others. Plates of cookies can be given to neighbors, enjoyed by the members or used as refreshments for each family to host their own Christmas party. Guests can bring their own containers to carry their cookies home in or else you could provide Christmas gift boxes for them to use. Set out a table where kids can decorate cookies, make gingerbread men and houses and make ornaments made out of cinnamon dough and shaped with cookie cutters. Find gospel-oriented cookie cutters or design your own by carefully bending metal sheets. Have a gingerbread house-building event or gingerbread man decorating contest. Invite everyone to share their favorite Christmas memory or story. Give everyone a cookie cutter attached to a ribbon as an ornament to take home.

December 7 — Pearl Harbor Day

◆ Use some of the patriotic ideas listed under Memorial Day in May and Veterans Day on November 11. You could also combine them with the Hawaiian décor ideas found under May 1st. Honor any ward members who were there that day.

December 12 — Poinsettia Day

◆ More poinsettia plants will be sold in North America in the six weeks before Christmas than all others combined in a year! If you're lucky enough to live near a Poinsettia nursery it would be fun to get a tour of their facility as a group. This could be a lovely theme for a Christmas dinner. To learn about this holiday plant from Mexico go to www.gardenersnet.com/flower/poinset.htm

December 13 — Cocoa Day

+ Decorate with mugs, chocolate, and marshmallows during a Christmas party to celebrate hot cocoa. Set out a Cocoa Bar so people can try different flavored syrups and toppings. Buy inexpensive plastic mugs so people can decorate them with markers. Provide ingredients so people can create one of those "Brownie mixes in a mug" gifts to take home. (For directions go to www.ehow.com/how_18589_make-brownies-jar.html) Set out melted chocolate, sprinkles, nuts and colored sugars for people to dip plastic spoons in and use in their hot chocolate.

+ Have a Christmas Cantata, inviting choirs from other wards and individuals to perform with yours and set out a chocolate fountain to feature Cocoa Day. Provide all kinds of munchies on skewers for dipping such as Rice Krispy squares, bananas, strawberries, cream puffs, cookies, pineapple, apple slices, Biscotti, peanut butter fudge, pound cake cubes, Angel Food cake, etc.

December 14 — South Pole Discovered, 1911

+ Decorate the party space like a polar exploration center with tents, snow shoes, skis, backpacks, lanterns, etc. You could feature penguins and use some of the ideas found on January 19.

December 16 — Maple Syrup Day

+ Have a Christmas breakfast, featuring different flavors of syrup on pancakes, waffles or French toast. Decorate the party space like a cozy Bed and Breakfast or lodge in Vermont with lots of quilts, logs, boots, trees, maple leaves, fake snow, farmhouses, and flannel. To make lots of Vermont trees soak pinecones in water overnight. Decorate tuna cans or butter tubs with paint, contact paper or ribbon. Fill can with sand and bury pinecones deeply enough that they stand upright. Sprinkle rye-grass seeds between petals of cones while they are wet. Keep sand wet and, each day, sprinkle cones with water. Grass will sprout in a few days.

December 22 — First Day of Winter

+ Throw a formal Winter Ball. Have a "Festival of Trees" theme where families can enter a tree-decorating contest and showcase them at the Winter Ball, awarding prizes to the winners. Glue glitter to the tips of pinecones. Kids make icicle ornaments by adding silver beads to a silver chenille pipe cleaner.

December 23 — Joseph Smith's birthday, 1805

+ Have a birthday party honoring the Prophet Joseph Smith.

December 25 — Christmas

+ There are TONS of craft and activity ideas for celebrating Christmas at:

> www.sabine.k12.la.us/ZES/christmassites/default.htm
> www.imagitek.com/xmas/crafts/
> www.dltk-holidays.com/xmas/index.html
> www.familycrafts.about.com/od/christmascrafts/
> www.enchantedlearning.com/crafts/christmas/
> www.allcrafts.net/xmas.htm
> www.craftown.com/xmas.htm
> www.njwebworks.net/christmas
> www.christmas.com

+ Encourage everyone to bring their nativity sets to display. This could become a huge community event or just a fun tradition for your ward members to enjoy. Provide a written card next to each display identifying what country the crèche is from or whose it is. One ward painted backdrops to go behind the displays, played Christmas music and had people walk by Christmas paintings in between the nativity sets for a longer show. Luminaries set outside on the walkways set the ambiance for a special evening.

+ Decorate the party space like a cruise ship and take a trip around the world, showcasing how other countries celebrate Christmas. Hang a banner that says Merry Christmas in different languages. Recruit the help of returned missionaries to set up booths that represent different countries, offering samples of food, music, crafts, language lessons, etc. Invite someone to share a short message entitled "Anchored to Christ" or "SOS" (Serve Our Savior) or "Sailing Home."

+ The popular "Night In Bethlehem" involves a lot of work but is quite powerful and memorable. Send out invitations to ward members, stating that a decree has gone out from Caesar for all to be taxed and to come to Bethlehem. As party guests arrive they will be greeted by a Census Taker who will give them gold coins in a rough muslin drawstring bag to spend at booths in exchange for paying taxes (bringing canned food that the ward will donate to a local food bank). You could also make salt dough coins. Encourage people to dress in "Biblical" attire or a simple bathrobe, tunic and head covering to help everyone really get into the mood. Create booths by building wooden 1 x 2 frames lashed together to tables and draping colored fabric or rough-looking muslin over them. Fill the room with fake palm trees or create roofs out of palm fronds. You can also make palm trees by painting cardboard tubes that come inside large rolls of carpet. You could have a formal program or simply allow families to wander at their leisure. Ask each auxiliary or different families to be in charge of creating and manning each booth during the evening. Here are some ideas to include in your event:

  + Create a stable outside with a live nativity display with Christmas music playing.
  + Serve pita pockets with roast beef, beef barley soup, falafel, grilled chicken skewers, herbed rice.
  + Have a bakery shop with baskets filled with rolls, flat breads, pita pockets, and Jewish Challah braided bread.
  + Make a cheese shop with different kinds to sample and see how it is made.
  + Have a booth that shows how to make rope or paper. Guests can try their hand at weaving on a loom.
  + Have a candle shop where guests can roll a beeswax candle.
  + Offer a dried and fresh fruit shop with different samples.

- Create a wood shop with displays and where guests could decorate a thin wood ornament. (Michaels and Oriental Trading Co. both have some.)

- Show guests how to play the dreidel game and give them one to take home.

- Build a well by using a big trash can and covering the outside with real stones or butcher paper painted to look like stones. You could also tape corrugated poster strips that look like brick, found in teacher supply stores. Assign a costumed character to offer dips of drink to guests.

- Have three people dress as kings to walk around with gold, frankincense and myrrh, asking people if they know where the baby king is. The gold is small rocks sprayed with gold paint. The frankincense is potpourri and the myrrh is slightly burned caramelized sugar broken into pieces.

- Set up a petting area outside with real pigmy goats, sheep, horses and cows, if possible.

- Make a Christmas tree ornament.

- Make a nice backdrop where guests can take their pictures dressed in time-period costumes.

- Serve roasted potatoes or corn on a stick.

- Show a movie about the nativity in one of the rooms.

- Create a sitting area in a covered tarp area where people can sit and visit, calling it the "Bethlehem Holiday Inn."

- Guests could make a 3-D star by connecting cardboard or Styrofoam star sheets together. Spray paint the sheets gold, add glitter and put a slit in the bottom of each one so the guests can slide them together. People could personalize them if they want by writing their names, the event date, and what gift they'll give to Jesus this year.

- Create a Hebrew School booth where "students" sit on blankets and learn to write Hebrew words with a quill on a scroll. Attach pencils to feathers for the quills and roll paper onto dowels for the scrolls. You can find out your name in Hebrew at www.my-hebrew-name.com/

- + Paint the skyline of the city of Bethlehem on butcher paper to hang on the walls or use masking tape to draw an outline of the city.
- + Set out battery-operated candles on tables.
- + Set out luminaries along the pathways outside.
- + Make a store with olives, jerky, dried figs, and almonds.

+ Create a "Santa's Workshop" so ward members can repair toys to donate to shelters, orphanages, the ward nursery and hospitals.

+ Make bell chimes out of pieces of pipe cut to certain lengths and have the Primary children sing and perform songs.

+ Invite Santa to come and teach the children about the symbols of Christmas. Have a wreath-decorating contest. You could serve meatloaf cooked in bundt pans to look like wreaths.

+ Families could decorate and fill one Christmas stocking to exchange with another at the party. When families arrive they put their stocking on a table and receive a number. Later the numbers are drawn for each stocking and presented to the families. *have the stockings be table dec. and families bring things to fill stick*

+ Organize your talented ward members and perform the wonderful Christmas musical *The Forgotten Carols* by Michael McLean. *for giving free.*

+ Have a "Kris Kringle Mingle" where you use a "Storybook Christmas" for your party theme. Decorate each dinner table using items from popular Christmas stories ("A Christmas Carol", "Twas the Night Before Christmas", "Twelve Days of Christmas", "The Gift of the Magi", "The Nutcracker", etc). Make the entrance look like guests are walking into a story book by painting the pages of a book out of butcher paper or cardboard from furniture boxes to make it look more sturdy. Decorate the stage to look like a cozy living room and have a few families sit on the stage set to share their favorite Christmas story or poem with the ward. Check out the LDS version of "Twas The Night Before Christmas" at www.of-worth.com/christmasprogram. htm for your ward to perform. Some families read one story each night while a candle burns down to another mark as a type

wise Men

of advent, so one of the crafts could be to mark special candles for the families to take home. For tons of stories check out:

www.allthingschristmas.com/stories.html

www.joyfulheart.com/christmas/

www.infostarbase.com/tnr/xmas/

www.inspirationalstories.com/christmas-1.html

• Have a traditional Christmas dinner program where the Primary children act out the nativity story and everyone sings Christmas carols. A silly way to liven up the song "Jingle Bells" is to divide the audience into 3 groups. Each group has to sing an assigned word when the music director points at them (Ding, Dong, and Dum). Put snacks on little sleds at each table. Kids could make advent calendars if your party is held early in December. Pass out a Christmas survey as an icebreaker that asks "Have you ever…" and awards points for each thing a person has done. The party guest with the most points is designated as the Ward Christmas Angel (give them a little angel ornament). The one with the least points is the Christmas Grinch (or Scrooge). Here are a few suggestions for your survey:

GIVE YOURSELF ONE POINT IF YOU HAVE EVER...

____ Gone over the river and through the woods to Grandma's house

____ Eaten an entire piece of Mincemeat Pie (not just a taste)

____ Had eggnog Mormon style

____ Eaten fruitcake

____ Eaten Figgy Pudding

____ Walked a mile in the snow to school

____ Worn a snowsuit

____ Gone snow skiing

____ Broken an arm or leg while skiing

____ Made a snowman

____ Made a snowwoman

____ Gone cross country skiing

____ Walked in snow shoes

____ Made an angel in the snow

____ Seen the movie "Snow Dogs"

____ Lost one mitten

____ Had a snowball fight

____ Made a snow fort

____ Tasted snow

____ Shoveled snow off the driveway or sidewalk

____ Scraped ice off your windshield

____ Eaten yellow snow

____ Had to breathe vapor from a hot bowl with a towel over your head

____ Hung icicles one by one on your Christmas tree instead of throwing them all on

____ Made a garland of popcorn and cranberries

____ Had an angel on the top of your tree

____ Had real lit candles on your Christmas tree

____ Gotten all your Christmas shopping done before Dec 1st

____ Opened your gifts on Christmas Eve

____ Got a lump of coal because you were bad

____ Heard Santa's sleigh on your roof

____ Hung your stocking on the couch because you didn't have a fireplace

• Another Christmas event that takes a lot of planning, but is very memorable is to recreate a Dickens Village where party guests can visit shops, listen to wandering carolers, make crafts and "purchase" items with gold coins in a drawstring bag they receive when they first arrive. Shops can be created by separating areas in the Cultural Hall with lattice boards and attaching 1x 2's to tables with a fabric awning over the top. You could also decorate individual rooms in the church building. Here are some items to consider including:

  • Set out real street lamps or create some by hanging lanterns on black-painted cardboard rolls that come inside carpet.

+ Have a Toy Shoppe where guests can see antique toys and make little rag dolls to donate to a shelter and one to keep.

+ Create a Post Office where guests write letters to the missionaries that will be included in a care package from the ward and make rubber stamped gift tags people can take home to use on their Christmas gifts. Make mailboxes or slots with the names of each of the missionaries and military servicemembers where people can put their letters.

+ Create "The Abbey." Paint stained glass windows on cardboard doors to enter a "church" where nativity sets are displayed from around the world.

+ Invite Father Christmas to wander the streets, giving small gifts to the children.

+ Have a Sweet Shoppe where guests pull taffy, make caramel apples, stir fudge, wrap "lollies" to take home or dip fruit in chocolate.

+ Make a Bakery where guests can sample meat pies, rolls, or make gingerbread houses out of graham crackers.

+ Have a Gift Shoppe where people bring mittens or socks to donate to a shelter.

+ Create Tiny Tim's Tiny Train Museum where there are train displays, plus some toy trains for kids to play with.

+ Create a park setting with benches and lots of plants where people can just sit and visit or listen to performers play a violin or harp.

+ Have an Inn with a fireplace and cozy chairs and couches where people can site and visit. Paint Victorian home scenes on butcher paper to hang for the "walls" and set up a picket fence around the outside.

+ Paint English countryside scenes on butcher paper to hang on the walls for an overall backdrop.

+ Recruit the help of a Town Crier who can wander through the "streets" and make random announcements in an English accent during the evening.

+ Have a traditional Christmas dinner at the Church building but here's a twist. Each dinner table is decorated with Dickens Christmas buildings and street scenes and standing next to each table is a tall (fake) street sign that has the name of an actual street near the church building. When the people seated at that table finish eating they are to go caroling to random houses on that particular street. When they finish singing, they are to invite the homeowners to join them back at the church for dessert and a Christmas message. The Bishopric can be dressed as the three Wise Men and give meaningful ornaments to all of the families to take home. Assign several families in your ward to be in charge of bringing their nativities from home to decorate one table each.

+ Using the "Nutcracker Ballet" as your theme, decorate each table with one of the different aspects of the ballet (Christmas tree, Sugar Plum fairy, Kingdom of Sweets, mice, soldiers, nutcrackers, etc.) The people sitting at each table have to come up with a skit, song, or dance that relates to their assigned table. If you have talented dancers in your ward you could have them perform a special number from the show. It would be cute to have the Achievement Day girls dress as ballerinas and perform something special together.

+ Decorate your party in the style of "The Polar Express" with train sets, robes, and bells. People are given a special ticket in order to get on to the train. Set up tables as if they are inside a dining train area. Give everyone a bell to take home at the end of the evening. Make giant trains out of cardboard appliance boxes and set out as many other trains as you can borrow from ward members.

+ Read the book "Christmas Jars" by LDS author Jason Wright and create a Christmas dinner that inspires ward members to do service for others. Decorate each table with mason jars and hang those twinkling white lights. Each family could fill a mason jar with treats and gifts to exchange with another at the party. When families arrive they set their mason jars on a table and are given a number. Later, numbers are called out and families are presented with a filled jar to take home. To learn more about the book, the author and projects around the country go to www. christmasjars.com

+ Re-create the Christmas story in the style of the Book of Mormon. See the book entitled "A NIGHT WITHOUT DARKNESS" written by Timothy Robinson.

+ Set out a "Giving Tree" in the foyer at church in November with the intent to request volunteers to donate Christmas gifts for families in need. Hang tags or special ornaments on the branches representing family members and their ages, clothing sizes, shoe sizes, and whether they're male or female. No names should be listed. The volunteer takes the tag or ornament to later attach it to his donation. Inform volunteers when and where their wrapped donations should be dropped off so the bishop can deliver them. When someone wants to buy a gift for that person he takes the ornament to remind himself of his commitment and then fills out a donor card with his own contact information and puts it into a specially decorated box. That way you can remind him, collect the item, send a thank you card, etc.

+ Go "Snowball Caroling." Assign several families to go caroling to less active members and encourage them to join the group, creating a snowball effect of people. Then all the groups meet together at one house or at the church building for refreshments. Invite a local high school's choir to perform.

+ Use the theme "JOY" for your Christmas event with someone giving a special presentation on what JOY stands for: J= Jesus, O=Others, Y=Yourself. Decorate wood block ornaments that say JOY and stack giant blocks made out of cardboard boxes that spell JOY to kind of look like toys. Have everyone do three activities, one that focuses on JESUS, a service project where they do something for OTHERS, and make a craft they can make for YOURSELF. Invite someone to share a short message entitled "A Season Of Joy" to talk about the different seasons of our lives.

December 26 — Boxing Day

+ Have everyone bring their gift boxes and big cardboard boxes they received their gifts in for Christmas and slide down some hills on top of the boxes. Everyone brings a box lunch for an outdoor picnic. Play the White Elephant game so people can trade the lousy gifts they got for Christmas.

December 31 — New Year's Eve

+ Encourage everyone to wear crazy hats and bring board games to share. Play some of the games from the chapter on ice breakers and mixers. Decorate with horn blowers, clocks, Baby New Year/Old Man Time, and confetti (make sure you have a good clean-up crew). Have a Baby New Year drawing contest. Hang netting on the ceiling filled with balloons that can then be dropped at the time you declare to be midnight. Have a table set out where children can make their own noisemakers, by filling beans and rice in plastic drink bottles or putting beans or beads inside two paper plates stapled together. Ask a Hallmark store to give you a bunch of their free little calendars to pass out to your party guests as a take-home gift. Create special calendars for the upcoming year that have pictures of different temples for each month and include a written reminder of the operating hours for your closest temple. You could celebrate midnight at 8:00 so the little ones can enjoy the fun. Decorate with clocks that show midnight. Give awards to ward members to celebrate momentous events that occurred during the past year (new babies, oldest ward member, newly baptized children and adults, missionaries who returned home, etc.) Set up a bunch of toasters for people to use with different kinds of bread. Have each family hold up a piece of toast and make a "toast" to the ward. Blow up balloons and put small pieces of paper in them that give good fortunes for the new year.

+ Have a New Year's Eve dance in the evening and serve breakfast after midnight.

CHAPTER 14

Ward Traditions That Unite The Heart

"What an enormous magnifier is
tradition! How a thing grows in the
human memory and in the human
imagination, when love, worship, and all
that lies in the human heart, is there to
encourage it."

THOMAS CARLYLE

Traditions can bind hearts together and create lasting memories. While some people view activities that are held annually as the glue that holds the ward family together, other people may view the same events as old and tired. Choose wisely. It's often difficult to create ward traditions because everyone changes callings so often and it's hard to find a sense of continuity. When you begin your new calling as Ward Activities Director make a quick phone call to your predecessor to find out what fun traditions may have been started. Likewise, when you are released, jot down some notes for the new person so he/she will have an idea of the legacy that you may have created. Of course, the new leader may choose not to carry on your great ideas, so don't be offended, but rather enjoy their fresh, new ideas and remember that we're all just trying to do our best!

Birthday Bricks

Find out when your building was first constructed and have a birthday party to honor its age. Celebrate the history of the ward and its members. You could have everyone sit at tables according to their birth month to encourage lots of mingling. Tables could be divided by the months of the year and decorated with monthly holiday items. Children could also be divided or all sit together at one table and color their placemats with birthday designs. Send the Prophet a birthday card from your ward. Roll out poster paper and have everyone sign it and then mail it to:

The Church of Jesus Christ of Latter-day Saints
Church Office Building
President's Office
50 E. North Temple
Salt Lake City, Utah 84150

Box of Love

Every month or quarter set out an empty box for each missionary, college student or military member who is serving far from home. Encourage the ward to bring items that can be sent, including non-perishable snacks, letters, cartoons, drawings, toiletries, etc. Tape record greetings from the people in the ward on to a cassette tape or make a salutations video on VHS or DVD.

Bust A Move

Have a contest in the ward to design a T-shirt that says something like "Bust A Move" that can be given to volunteers who show up to help new families move into the ward. You're sure to get a few more helpers and every so often you can hold "Bust A Move" special events for all of the members of that prestigious club.

Secret PAL (Performing Acts of Love)

Create Secret "PAL" cards that members can leave for one another when they've performed a secret service. Encourage "Random Acts of Kindness" that could be performed for family, neighbors and in the community. Groups within the ward could also do service for one another, such as the Achievement Day girls baking cookies for the Boy Scouts. It would be fun to see how creative everyone gets and would definitely provide a unifying spirit in your ward.

Survivor

Make "Welcome To The Area!" packets for new move-ins. Include maps of the area, phone numbers, a ward directory, school and utility information, Parks and Recreation catalogs, coupons to local stores, a hometown newspaper, information on church meeting and activity schedules, etc.

Golden Apple Award

Some wards and stakes have a terrific tradition of presenting local high school teachers, Seminary teachers, or favorite coaches with a special apple award at a fancy dinner. The evening could include guest speakers, slide show, entertainment, and youth choir. It's a wonderful tradition that creates goodwill in the community and helps the youth express their gratitude while representing the high standards of the Church. You could also include teachers from elementary and middle schools. Be sure to invite community leaders from the school board, city government and even the press.

Adopt A Mile

Talk to your local city government about their "Adopt A Mile" program and how your ward could get involved. You will need to commit to cleaning up a certain stretch of a road or waterway for an extended length of time. Be sure to get approval from your bishop. You could involve the entire ward by assigning special clean-up days or by rotating auxiliaries throughout the year to help with this ongoing service project.

New To You Table

Set out a table where members can bring any of their unwanted items from home and others are free to take whatever they want. Items that still remain at the end of the night can be delivered to Goodwill or Deseret Industries or any other organization of your choosing. You could also deliver items to your local Spanish or Vietnamese branch (or whatever special needs branch you have in your area). You can have members bring random items each month or designate a different theme each month such as kitchen items, toiletries, children's items, clothing, etc.

Door Prizes

Door prizes are fun to use to help solve any problems you might be having at activities in order to reward positive behavior. For example, if the members have a tendency to straggle in late you could award door prizes to everyone who is there on time. If you want to encourage missionary work with the ward you could offer a little prize to each member who brings a friend to the activity. Door prizes could also be offered randomly to add a little excitement for the evening. Prizes don't have to cost much and can even be donated by local vendors. All you have to do is ask!

S.O.S Table

S.O.S stands for Seek Out Service. Each month one or two organizations are spotlighted so members can get ideas for service projects they can become involved in with their families or individually. This is an opportunity to introduce the members to ways they can become more involved in their community and reach out to others. You can leave pamphlets or flyers on the table that provide more information, including a contact phone number so the members can follow through.

Organizations you might want to introduce to your ward could include: The American Kidney Foundation, Second Harvest, American Cancer Society, local nursing homes they can visit or perform in, local hospitals they can volunteer, Special Olympics, Boys/Girls Clubs, Locks of Love, The Happy Factory, Care Wear, Crafting Angels, Project Linus, Newborns in Need, etc. Contact the Church's Humanitarian Department for ideas on dozens of service projects. Call (801) 240-6060 or e-mail HumanitarianCenter@lds church.org .

You can also check out www.lds.org/ldsfoundation/welfare Find out how you can help with the upcoming EFY service projects that might be held in your area during the next summer.

Ward Photo Directory

Digital cameras make putting together a photo directory a snap! Group families together, being careful to write the names in the correct order. An updated directory could be printed every year or so. The directory could include phone numbers and addresses of the members and missionaries, as well as hours for the closest temple and Family History Center. You will be impressed how much this one project can bring a ward closer.

Family Home Evening packet

Set out a table during each activity where families can put together a Family Home Evening packet to take home that reinforces the theme of the activity or a gospel principle you were incorporating into the event. A packet could include visual aids, a simple recipe for refreshments, songs that coordinate with the selected theme, and even a refrigerator magnet with a scripture. During the ward event, children can be kept busy coloring the pages provided for the lesson. The packets can be a nice activity to keep small hands busy during the party, as well as a nice take-home gift.

Happy Hammers

Sign up your ward to help build a Habitat for Humanity House in your community each time there is a project. Wear matching T-shirts to create both a sense of family in your ward, as well as a reputation in the community that Latter-day Saints are happy helpers. The members who can't do physical labor could provide lunches and snacks for workers or even sew curtains for the new homes. Check out www.habitat.org.

Toys For Tots

Gather and clean toys to donate to children in need during the holidays. Check out www.toysfortots.org Have members bring their children's old, ragged dolls and stuffed animals and have a toy workshop to repair and refresh them. If children have outgrown toys they could be donated to your church's nursery or a local children's group. You could bring out receptacles at each activity where people can place their donated items.

Get To Know You Table

Invite ward members to bring a few items to put on a table that describe themselves and their interests so that everyone can get to know them a little better. You could spotlight new move-ins only one month or a particular auxiliary.

The Babysitters Club

If you choose to have an adult's only activity you could create "The Babysitters Club" by awarding each helper that tends the children a ribbon, button or certificate that makes him/her an honorary member. Some time during the year you could host a party in honor of all the babysitters who have become members of this prestigious club.

UnBirthday Party

Have an "Unbirthday Party" just to celebrate everyone's birthday at once or just to break up the monotony of a long, cold winter. Each month you could spotlight members in the ward who have their birthday, by presenting them a special treat or paper crown to wear during the ward activity. Make a poster for your ward bulletin board that lists the names of everyone celebrating their birthday that month.

Adult Fireside

The youth get to go to monthly fireside discussions in someone's home, so why not the adults too? Serve refreshments in a casual setting and invite a speaker to give a presentation on some aspect of the gospel.

The Taste of Service

Share ideas on how your kitchen can bless others. Pass around a calendar to have members take turns bringing in meals for the busy Bishopric when they start doing Tithing Settlement appointments in November and December. If you don't have one already, pass around another sign-up sheet for members to make dinner appointments for the full-time missionaries. Offer to make sack lunches for all of the missionaries on transfer day or Zone Conference.

You CAN Do It

Plan an activity at your local Family Home Storage Center, Cannery or Bishop's Storehouse assignment. Provide samples of dishes prepared with food storage items.

The Door To A Bishop's Heart

Each month or quarter, decorate the bishop's door with thank you letters, pictures of families in the ward, or other fun items that remind him he is loved and appreciated. You could take pictures from previous ward activities or have children draw pictures. Your ward committee could put the decorations together or else you could assign a different auxiliary to do it each month until everyone has had an opportunity.

Spotlight on the Saints

Each month a different family is spotlighted and given a little gift. Invite the family to stand in front of the group while you tell all about their favorite things, accomplishments and talents, and why they are so special to the ward. You could also tell the group all about them and have the ward try to guess who they think it is and then invite the family to stand. Be sure to include the singles in your ward.

Cozy Corner

Create a quiet corner somewhere in the building during your activity where ward members can take turns reading books or Church magazines aloud and recording them on tape to loan to the older members who have poor eyesight and can't read any more. You could also create a library of tapes for people to check out, such as for those who spend a lot of time in their cars.

Greenies

Honor new families and individuals who have moved into your ward since the last ward activity by presenting them a token gift, crown, or green "Miss America" type of banner to wear during the event.

Recipe Book

Create a ward cookbook, gathering family favorites in various categories such as appetizer, beverages, dessert, main dish, salad, bread, etc. To kickstart the effort you could hold a big tasting event or contest. You could also encourage ward members to create their own ward cookbook by simply handing out the recipes at each activity for the refreshments or meals that were served.

Theme

Choose a theme for each year such as "Building the Kingdom" or "Building Celestial Families." All of the activities would be designed to reinforce that particular theme.

Break the Fast

If the building schedule allows, hold a potluck dinner after Fast Sunday services where everyone can end their fast together and enjoy fellowship with one another. Award the best dishes in various food categories with a "Golden Spoon" award. Encourage families to donate one canned food item as their ticket into the event and then take the donations to a local food shelter or to help a family in need in the ward.

It's a good reminder on Fast Sunday to serve others and that the money we would have spent on meals is to help others in need. Invite one of the auxiliary organizations to supply some musical entertainment each month.

Sister City

Go to www.lds.org to locate another ward somewhere in the world you could become ward Pen Pals with. Try to find a "Sister City" ward with a similar name you could correspond with and exchange fun care packages with.

Choose The Write

Create a summer reading rewards program by challenging families to read the scriptures (or other good books) and awarding those who read 100 pages or more with a special treat or prize.

Park Pals

Invite families to gather at a local park to play and visit once a month after school or on a Saturday. It can be an informal get-together or you could provide games and snacks.

Open Gym

During the cold, winter months or even during the hot and humid ones, open up the gym at the church building for families to play indoor games and visit. It can be an informal get-together or you could provide games and snacks.

FHE 101

Once a year hold a ward Family Home Evening at the church building. It's a fun way to introduce newer members how to hold Family Home Evening, and a nice reminder to everyone that the ward can be like another family to them.

Ward Roadshow

While you're waiting for your stake to organize a youth Roadshow event, you could invite families to put together skits or musical plays for your very own annual Ward Roadshow. If you have a lot of talent in your ward you could create an entire production of one the old Church classics such as *Saturday's Warrior* or *My Turn on Earth*.

I Could Have Danced All Night

Some areas of the Church have incredible Dance Festivals where youth perform musical shows with a variety of dance styles. If you don't have this fun tradition in your area, start one! Families could be invited to prepare dance numbers or you could encourage each auxiliary to put together a particular routine. A great theme to work with is "World of Dance" with international numbers and a look at how the Church is growing in different countries.

Speech & Debate Tournament

Some Stakes hold an annual Speech & Debate Tournament to help the youth improve their public speaking skills. If your stake doesn't provide such an opportunity, you could create a family event by creating fun categories and judges who offer helpful advice and light-hearted awards. Participants can enter a 5-minute speech in categories such as "High Council Highlights", "Stand-Up Comedy", "Book of Mormon Toasts", etc.

Empty Nesters

If your ward has a lot of older folks in it, you could offer a monthly Family Home Evening just for them, fun field trips, or restaurant excursions.

See Sister Jane Run

If your area has a famous marathon and your ward has a lot of runners you could create a fun celebration event after the annual run by honoring those who participated in the race. It could be as simple as a BBQ where the runners get to wear their prestigious, new race T-shirts. Hold a "Diaper Dash" for the babies and offer healthy food to encourage more members to get fit.

The Ward Word

Create a ward newsletter or encourage the bishop to call someone to do this. Even a simple monthly publication can have a great unifying effect on a ward. Hold a contest to see who can come up with the best name for the newsletter. Some items to include each month or quarter are: calendar items, releases, new callings, lesson schedules, priesthood advancements, births, deaths, baptisms, new move-ins, big anniversaries, birthdays, upcoming events in the ward and stake, etc. Ask each of the auxiliaries to send you information each month and include lots of candid pictures of people at past events.

Guess Who's Coming to Dinner

Anyone who wants to participate can sign up and volunteer to either host a dinner at their house or bring food items as a guest. You may have only one group of enthusiastic diners or several homes that can then meet at one location afterwards for dessert. It can be a more formal adults-only dinner or else a casual family-style event.

Temple Trek

If you don't live near a temple you may want to plan a big ward trek to the temple. Prepare activities for the children to keep them busy and happy while the adults attend endowment sessions and the youth perform baptisms. Families can bring picnic items to share at a nearby park afterwards. If you live near a temple, choose one day a month when ward members could attend the temple together during the day time and at night time.

This Is Your Life

When a new Bishopric has been called in your ward, be sure to create a special activity where you can honor the released men who served so well, as well as get to know the new ones coming in. Set out tables where you can display pictures and items from their lives. Present the past Bishopric members with a scrapbook filled with photos and letters of thanks from ward members.

The Gift of Life

Call 1-800-GIVELIFE or your local blood bank to find out how your ward and/or stake could host an annual blood drive.

Gratitude In Deed

Once every year or quarter, set out tables with stationery where people can write letters of gratitude to the First Presidency, Temple Presidency, Stake Presidency., or Mission Presidency in your area.

Temple Pageant

If one is available in your area, attend a Temple Pageant together as a ward. Most are held during summer months, but a few are offered during other seasons such as Easter and Christmas. Get directions and scheduled times online.

Some shows include the Mesa Easter Pageant, "And It Came To Pass" Oakland temple pageant, Hill Cumorah Pageant in Palmyra, New York, "The Mormon Miracle" in Manti, Utah, "City of Gathering" in Kirtland, Ohio. If you don't live close to any pageants you could show a video of the performance.

Scrapbooking Mania

At each activity create a staging area where families or individuals can have their pictures taken. The scrapbooking moms will be thrilled to be able to document the event.

Sweet Sixties

Spotlight the older members in your ward at an annual luncheon and share a little bit about their lives so the younger members can get to know them. Your "Golden Oldies" can be a tremendous resource for leadership ideas and experiences. They can also give you great ideas for successful ward activities they have seen over the years!

Meet And Greet

Each year invite a local author to speak to the members about his/her book and talk about the process of writing and the experience of getting something published.

The author could be LDS or not. You could also hold an annual event where you invite and meet local government leaders.

Ward Yearbook

Begin a ward scrapbook for your ward. Take pictures at each month's activity. You might even encourage the bishop to call someone to serve as the "Ward Historian." If your ward activity or service project is especially awesome, be sure to submit photos and a letter to the Church Magazines Department and your ward might get into the next publication! Send information about your special activity to:

LDS Church Magazines
50 East North Temple
SLC, UT 84150

Secret Saints

One month before an activity, any time of year, have each family pick another family's name out of a hat to determine who will be a "Secret Saint" for whom. During the next few weeks the families can do all kinds of anonymous service and make little gifts for one another. You may want to establish certain guidelines that limit the dollar amount of spending to encourage members to be more creative and so it won't be a financial burden. At the ward activity have all of the Secret Saints reveal themselves to each other. Often times there will be members who go all out while others don't do very much. Be sure that it is a voluntary experience so that only the families who really get excited about this idea will participate, while others who don't want to do it can gracefully slip out.

Waters of Mormon

Honor newly baptized members in your ward, whether they be adults or Primary children. Give them a packet that includes copies of Church magazines, pictures of Christ, a ward directory, tithing envelope, calendar of upcoming events, and a special note from the bishop, congratulating them on their decision to be baptized and welcoming them into the ward family.

I Love A Parade

Decorate a float for your local parade. Organize clowns and performers who will walk with your float and perform.

Say Cheese!

Set out disposable cameras on each table or scattered throughout the room so that ward members can take pictures of each other throughout the activity. Let them know you will develop the film and then post them on the ward bulletin board or web site for everyone to see. Set up a digital camera station where you can take pictures of ward members during the party and then print them out as a take-home gift.

The Binder That Binds

Each month a family is chosen to take home a binder that has a special questionnaire or simply blank pages. The family answers the questions and/or decorates a blank page to tell about themselves. They then pass the binder on to another family next month. To speed up the process and fill the binder faster you could pass it around each week. Questions to be answered could include things about the family's interests, accomplishments, traditions or testimonies.

CHAPTER 15

Feeding His Sheep

"Enchant, stay beautiful and graceful,
but do this, eat well. Bring the same
consideration to the preparation of your
food as you devote to your appearance.
Let your dinner be a poem, like your
dress."

CHARLES PIERRE MONSELET
French author (1825-1888) Letters to Emily

Food Tips

You have to realize that some people come to a ward activity just for the free food! A good rule of thumb is better to have more than not enough. If you and your committee have the freezer space you can store leftovers for the next event. You can always give the leftovers to the missionaries or to families in need. You could ask the bishop or Relief Society's Compassionate Service Coordinator to take leftovers to people who need help. Bring extra gallon-size baggies or containers so you can divide and package the food to give away at the end of the night.

+ Provide on each table some bowls of nuts, chips, crudités, popcorn, bread, crackers, cheese trays, antipasto, or something for your guests to snack on while they wait for the main course. Be creative and make the containers complement your theme by lining various clean items with tissue paper or cellophane before filling with snacks: shoes, sand pails, small umbrellas, paint cans, hats, flower pots, etc.

+ To help calculate the correct food quantities:

> MEAT : Figure about 4 to 8 oz raw meat per person. When the meat is cooked you will have about 1/2 to 2/3 of the original size. If you have more children than adults then you won't need as much meat. If you have more adults than children you'll probably want a little bit more. When checking amounts for meat you'll need to consider the water and bone weight in the total package.

> SALADS: You'll need about 1/2 cup of lettuce per adult for a tossed salad. Offer lots of salad for people to fill up on and to stretch the main course serving size. A 9 x 13 pan of Jell-O salad feeds 12 to 15 helpings.

> VEGETABLES: Plan on 1/2 cup per person.

> DESSERTS: Pies can be cut into 8 or 6 pieces, depending on if you are serving adults or children. Desserts made in a 9 x 13 pan will serve 12 to 15 people. Plan on 2 cookies per person.

> BREAD: Rolls and biscuits are great filler food. Plan on 2 per person. If guests are still hungry after eating the main course they can always eat another roll. Ask bakeries if they will donate their day-old bread to help stretch your budget.

+ Refreshments that are served could include something terribly decadent, as well as a "lighter" version of the same thing to help teach members how to cook with less fat and calories. Set out a sign next to the "Lighter Side" so people will understand it's a different recipe.

+ Most people like to try a little bit of everything when faced with a buffet. Smaller portions of food could be presented so that everyone can taste a variety of things without having to commit to a full-size helping. Feature appetizer sizes and you also won't see as much food going to waste. Call it a Taster's Table so people will be in the mindset that smaller portions are expected.

- To create an elegant feeling to your dinner, recruit the help of your committee or the Young Men and Young Women to walk around the room, offering appetizers on trays to party guests.

- Sometimes people don't seem to put much effort into their dishes when bringing something to share for a pot-luck, so you could offer prizes to motivate them to bring something extra special.

- Save money on paper products and use the actual dishes that your building has. Be sure to assign people to stay after the party to wash the dishes. This could be a great assignment for the High Priests!

- If you want to have a pot-luck, you're more likely to get a balanced meal if you assign certain items. For example, you could ask families whose names end A-G to bring entrées, H-K to bring salads, L-R to bring rolls or veggies, and S-Z to bring desserts. Another way to organize it is to ask Relief Society to bring entrees, Primary to bring dessert, Youth to bring salads, High Priests to bring rolls or veggies, and Elders Quorum to set up and clean up.

- Put out balls of dough to keep the kids busy, making their own culinary creations such as rolls, pretzels, or breadsticks. Save inexpensive pin tins so that you can send the children home with their dough to bake later.

- Provide markers near the cups so guests can write their names on their drinks and, hopefully, only use one during the evening rather than several.

- Make bundles of one napkin and utensils wrapped together with raffia or a ribbon and put them in a large basket for people to grab and go or at each place setting to ensure everyone has what they need.

- Everyone loves smoothies and shakes, so set out a station where people can have one made especially for them. This will take a LOT of ice and will be quite noisy, so make sure you have the help and the right set-up before attempting this one.

+ You can dress up a food table by designing your own specialty toothpicks. Print small pictures of an item that goes with your theme, cut them out and tape them to each toothpick. Place the toothpicks in fruit or veggie platters. You can also do the same thing with straws to dress them up.

+ Dress up drinks by simply inserting a sliced lemon or orange on the edge, attaching fruit to a toothpick or sticking a little umbrella in the cup.

+ Set out a menu at each place setting with very gourmet-sounding names for the dishes, even though the meal may be simple, to add a fine dining flair. For example, instead of chicken and potatoes say something like "herb-infused chicken baked in a rosemary-fired brick oven with french roasted garlic potatoes de jour.

+ Dress up any platter of food by simply placing attractive lettuce leaves underneath. You can also use a bed of flowers, non-toxic plant leaves, lemon slices or decorate strips of bread.

+ Just for fun at each meal activity you have, set out a Taster's Table for people to vote on which undisclosed sample they like the best and then give the results of the poll at the end of the party. Items you could have people vote on could be butter vs. margarine, store-bought milk vs. food storage milk, whole wheat brownies vs. regular brownies, sourdough bread vs. regular bread, etc.

+ Borrow one of those chocolate fountains or beverage fountains so people have to linger longer at the refreshment table and talk. Beware, while they're fun and yummy, they are very messy.

+ When passing around food sign-up sheets at Church, be sure to specify food categories on the list such as green salad, veggie side-dishes, rolls, appetizers, etc. otherwise everyone will show up with a bag of chips or you'll end up with a million Jell-O salads. For example, if you need 5 salads then make 5 lines where people can sign their name and phone number. Have someone on your committee be sure to call the volunteers as a reminder and thank them for their help. You may even want to bring a small gift to those who helped bring food or stuck around to help you clean up.

- Have people decorate their own cookies so they stay and mingle longer.

- During potlucks, set out small bowls of snacks, veggies, or fruit so hungry people will be able to wait more patiently until it's their turn to get in line.

- Begin "Amish Friendship Bread" by creating a starter dough that is then passed on to another and then another.

- Serve different food items on each table and when a bell rings everyone can get up and change tables to sample the other foods. This will shake up their table companions as well and keep conversations fresh.

- Provide each table with a bag to make "Friendship Fudge". Combine the following ingredients together in a gallon-sized baggie and have the guests at each table take turns gently squeezing the bag when it comes to them. Talk about how the rewards are sweet when we work together. Each table can then eat their dessert when ready.

4 cups powdered sugar
3 ounces softened cream cheese
1/2 cup softened margarine
1/2 cup cocoa
1 tsp. vanilla
1/2 chopped nuts

THE TEN COMMANDMENTS OF SUCCESSFUL POTLUCKS
(author unknown)

1. Thou shalt bring plenty of food that thy plate may be full, and thy brother's also.

2. Thou shalt use thy good manners so as not to appear as the beasts in the field.

3. Thou shalt remember the sabbath day and not run around like crazy in the cultural hall or other parts of the building.

4. Thou shalt leave thy comfort zone and talk to someone you don't know that thou might have the joy of a new friend.

5. Thou shalt stay in thy third-hour meetings until the final "Amen" that the spirit may abound.

6. Thou shalt be mindful that the people in the back of the line need food too, so please take small servings and then thou canst return for seconds after all have been served.

7. Thou shalt eat only in the cultural hall, for it is forbidden to wander about with food and it is most abominable to eat in the classrooms, lest a mess shall follow thee and the whole building be smitten with a curse of crumbs and gunk.

8. Thou and thy family shall wait with patience and cheerfulness until it is thy turn in line.

9. Many shall eat and many shall clean up after themselves that all might go home rejoicing.

10. Thou shalt bring a friend to join us next time, both the Jew and the Gentile, that all might be edified and receive physical and spiritual food.

Food Themed Parties

"Mormon Bar"

Create a bar that Mormons can actually go to! There are so many different kinds you can create and it allows people to eat what they actually like. Set out a variety of toppings so people can create their own edible masterpiece.

Another version of this is to play a game where the members have to answer questions about the gospel, recite the Articles of Faith, donate a canned food item or toy, or do anything else you want them to before they can get another topping. The more questions they answer correctly the more toppings they get! Another version is if they answer the question correctly they get to roll some dice. The numbers on the dice correspond to various items: napkin, fork, cup, plate, and the various food ingredients. As they answer questions correctly they begin to accumulate the items from the bar and can eat once they have all been gathered. Types of "bars" to consider serving are:

BAKED POTATOES: chili, cheeses, onions, sour cream, bacon bits, chives, butter, veggies

SWEET POTATOES: cinnamon, sugars, butter, marshmallows, chocolate chips

TACOS, BURRITOS, NACHOS: cheeses, lettuce, tomatoes, green onions, black beans, corn, olives, chilis, sauces, sour cream, meat, peppers, refried beans, pinto and kidney beans

PITA BREAD SANDWICHES: lettuce, meats, tomatoes, peppers, sprouts, cucumbers, jicama, sauces, condiments, purple onions, sliced veggies, falafels

BUILD A SUBWAY SANDWICH: different breads and meats, lettuce, avocado, tomato, sprouts, pickles, condiments, purple onions, sauces, bacon strips

SALAD BAR: veggies, fruits, crunchy toppings, assortment of other kinds of salads like 3 bean salad, potato salad, pasta salad, fruit salad, warm spinach salad, etc.

SMOOTHIE STATION: ice, fruit, juices, chopped veggies

MUFFIN BAR: different kinds of muffins, cinnamon rolls, flavored butters, variety of jams and jellies

OMELET STATION: cheeses, egg whites only as an option, cheeses, sauces, chopped vegetables, salsa

POUND CAKE STATION: fruit, whip cream, chocolate, flavored syrups, nuts, caramel

ICE CREAM SUNDAE: nuts, candies, whip cream, sauces, bananas, syrups, sprinkles, waffle cones

SOUP: veggies, crackers, breads, cheeses, crunchy toppings, cooked rice, noodles

TAPAS: a million different kinds of appetizers and sauces

MONGOLIAN BBQ: cooked meats, cooked veggies, different kinds of sauces, chow mein noodles, rice, Chinese veggies

ENGLISH DESSERT TRIFLE AND PARFAITS: puddings, custards, fruit, angel food cake, pound cake, whip cream, nuts, sauces and syrups, angel fingers, cookies

Carnival

Have booths where guests have to complete tasks or games to earn prizes. Fun and simple tasks might include answering a Church history quiz, reciting scriptures or Articles of Faith, "Name that Face" game using pictures of members in your ward, matching temples with locations, or you could even have them come up with clever missionary door approaches to earn prizes. Use gospel twists to traditional carnival games like Ring Toss, Bowling, Bean Bag toss, fishing for a prize. Members are given tickets to spend at booths to "buy" refreshments.

"Chef's Night"

Decorate with a kitchen or bistro theme and be sure to have everyone on your committee wear Chef hats. You could also have a table set out where the children can make their own chef hat out of paper. Go to www.familyfun.com for instructions to make a really cute poofy, white chef's hat. You could also give one to each guest as they enter the party. Hang kitchen items from doorways, as centerpieces and around the food table. Set out pictures of famous chefs or fancy dishes. This event could be a food tasting party, a potluck dinner, a cooking contest, or a fully prepared dinner for guests. Some activities to include in the festivities could be:

- Play 20 questions (guess foods and kitchen objects)
- Bean toss into jars or candy toss into muffin pans
- Guess flavors of food items, baby food, or spices
- Have guests design and laminate personal placemats
- Guess the missing object (remove one object at a time from a large display of kitchen gadgets)
- Toss pizza dough in the air contest
- Hot potato (using real warm potato)
- Relay races (using real foods or kitchen gadgets)
- Match names and photos of famous chefs
- Read food-themed books (Green Eggs and Ham, In the Night Kitchen)
- Make pasta or dried bean mosaics

- Make picture collages of favorite foods on one half of the poster and least favorite foods on the other half
- Identify herbs and spices game
- Make personalized pot holders by decorating with fabric paints
- Decorate cookies or cupcakes

"How Have You Bean?

Have a cooking contest or potluck dinner where everyone has to bring dishes prepared with food storage items. Offer prizes for the most creative items and provide samples of items from the Family Home Storage Center (the Cannery) such as dried applies, refried bean flakes, etc. Ask families to submit copies of their best recipes so you can hand out a Food Storage cookbook as a take-home gift.

"You Take The Cake!"

The Young Women and Scouts are always looking for ways to earn money for their summer camps and trips. Assign them to bake and decorate special cakes and then hold an auction after your dinner.

"One Dish Wonders"

To throw an interesting twist on a typical pot-luck dinner, invite everyone to bring food items that are prepared in only one dish, such as a casserole or crock-pot. Gather recipes and share the cookbook with the ward to help them with easy Sunday cooking ideas.

"Talk the Wok"

Invite the members to bring meats and veggies that can be cooked in a wok. Set up stations around the room where they can watch their food being cooked up as a stir-fry. Offer eggrolls, dipping sauces, rice and noodles.

"It's A Wrap!"

This meal is all about cooking with tortillas, gyros, lettuce wraps, pita pockets, cabbage rolls and breadless sandwiches for Low Carbohydrate meals. Offer all kinds of cooked and deli meats.

"There's Always Room For Jell-O"

You could hold a contest to see how creative the members can be with gelatin to combat the reputation we Relief Society sisters have of serving only boring, green Jell-O at every dinner! Encourage members to use cute molds to create interesting shapes and layered gelatin dishes. Make fun, jiggly treats for the kids, hold a Jell-O slurping contest and dress someone up like Bill Cosby to visit the crowd.

"Sensational Salads"

You'll have to provide some meat for this event or else all of the men will revolt. Invite families to share their favorite kind of salad: fruit, green, pasta, etc. Set out a table of different kinds of toppings people can add to their salads such as Jicama, dried cranberries, glazed nuts, orange zest, spiced beans, Feta cheese, Gorgonzala or Bleu cheese crumbles, Tofu cubes, French-fried onions, etc. Give prizes for the most unusual salad, yummiest, fanciest, best dressed, etc. Discuss the Word of Wisdom. Be sure to share recipes!

"Sweet as pie" or "I Eta Pi"

Invite the members to bring anything that could be considered a pie, such as baked pies, meat pies, empanadas, Shepherd's pie, pot pies, Hot Pockets, and refrigerator cream pies. Mmmm You could use a Greek theme and initiate members into the "I Eta Pi" Club.

"Rice To The Occasion"

This event showcases everything you wanted to know about rice but were afraid to ask. Set out different kinds of rice such as pilaf, brown, steamed, fried, Japanese grain, and wild. Serve casseroles that use rice as a crust. Have children make mosaic art projects with rice.

"The Melting Pot"

Introduce the ward to an evening of fondue cooking. Set up tables with fondue pots that feature different styles of fondue meals such as cheese, white and dark chocolates, hot oils, chicken and beef broth, marshmallow crème, etc. Set out trays of dipping items like fruits, vegetables, crusty breads, meats, cheeses, candy, cookies, cakes, and nuts. To make sure people get enough to eat, set out another table with some tossed salads and rolls.

"Grandma's Grits and Grub"

Encourage ward members to bring potluck items that represent old family recipes. Decorate with old-fashioned kitchen décor and old photographs. Work with your Family History Specialist for ideas on how to combine this dinner event with genealogy games and activities.

"Berry Interesting"

This event is to celebrate the summer berry season. Provide cobblers, jams, sauces, fruit leather, salsas, strawberry shortcake, pies, and even spa items that feature berries. Play games like "Toss the Strawberry", races that involve carrying berries from one spot to another while blindfolded or on a spoon. Sew red bean bags with black spots and add green yarn on the top to look like strawberries and then have people toss them into buckets or through holes for prizes. Hold either a serious "Miss Berry" contest with a talent competition or else a goofy one with men from the Elders Quorum and have judges award points for the hairiest legs or baldest head, awarding the winner a crown and banner to wear.

"Soup's On!"

This activity is perfect for cold, winter nights. Invite ward members to share all different kinds of soups, served with an assortment of yummy rolls and breads. Set out a variety of soup toppings such as baked tortilla strips, oyster crackers, grilled veggie mix-ins, green onions, avocado, crispy onions, etc. Decorate with aprons and those old-fashioned, red Campbell soup labels.

"Great Grains"

Showcase a dinner where you can introduce ward members to all kinds of different grains such as kamut, teff, amaranth, flax, quinoa, hemp, faro as well as red and white wheat. Talk with your ward Food Storage Specialist for fun recipe ideas and activities that might interest the kids. Check out www.chefbrad.com (Every year he cooks dinner for his mission president and one of his companions, so maybe he'll cook me dinner if I mention him in this book.)

"Smooth As Ice"

Set up your own juice and smoothie bar to make blended drinks, Slurpies, Icees, Pina Coladas, and Daqueris (all virgin, of course). Set out one of those juicing machines and have people sample different blends of fruit and vegetables. Have your committee wear hats with fruit in them and hold a Carmen Miranda contest.

"Bon Appetit"

The Bon Appetit cooking magazine has a section where readers ask the Editor to convince restaurants to share recipes for some of their most popular items. Everyone wants to know how to make those yummy Mrs. Fields Chocolate Chip cookies, Red Lobster biscuits, or TGI Friday's Potato Skins. Invite ward members to bring "mock" versions of some of those favorites.

"Foiled Again!"

This is perfect for an outdoor picnic or campout. Set out tables with various ingredients for people to create their own "Hobo Packet" such as ground beef, onions, potatoes, carrots, celery, chicken, mushrooms, etc. Have them add spices and some condensed chicken or mushroom soup and the wrap everything up in foil, writing their name on the outside of the packet with permanent markers.

"Sweet Nothings" or "Sweet Shoppe"

The kids are gonna love this one! Showcase different kinds of candies. Guests can pull taffy or make chocolate. Set up one of those chocolate fountains where people can dip fruit, biscotti, cream puffs, Rice Krispy squares, and other things into the fountain. Set out containers with different sized candy and have people guess how many pieces are inside. You could even turn the event into a Willy Wonka theme and have the children sing and dance like Oompa Loompas. Decorate and advertise with candy grams. Make giant Hershey's kisses by shaping chocolate or rice krispie squares into a funnel and wrapping in foil. Create your own message on the white slip of paper that spills out of the kiss. Let people make their own lollipops and other confections.

Progressive dinner

If your ward boundaries include your church building you could either begin or end at the building. Hopefully you'll get lucky and find some members who live within walking distance to one another so you can have everyone walk to each house after each course. You can have separate houses for hors d'eourves, soup, salad, entrée, and dessert. You may want to limit house visits to just three homes if they're located farther away. If none of the members live close enough to each other to make it practical you could host a traveling dinner by using and decorating different rooms in your church building. Include a special talk, skit, or musical number during each course.

"Pizza Night!"

Feature different kinds of pizza: deep dish, vegetarian, fruit, dessert, thin crust, meat lovers, BBQ chicken, feta cheese and pesto sauce with veggies, etc. Showcase different kinds of crust too: Boboli, hand-made, Bisquick, cookie, etc. Have a contest where participants have to design something out of pizza dough as well as a good old-fashioned pizza toss. Decorate with an Italian flair and give prizes to ward members who speak with Italian accents during the evening. Ask your local pizza restaurants to donate balls of dough, pizza boxes or certificates to use as prizes.

"By Their Fruits Ye Shall Know Them"

This is an especially fun activity in the summer time and combines well with a luau, pool party, or picnic. Showcase all kinds of fruit. Serve fruit salad, ambrosia, fruit kabobs, grilled pineapple, chocolate dipped frozen bananas, fruit salsa, jams, sorbets, creamy sauces for dipping, and smoothies. Get creative by cutting them in fun shapes. Have the children make funny faces using different fruit pieces on a plate. Scoop out the insides of oranges, melons, lemons, pineapples and coconuts to use as serving bowls. Play relay games where people have to run with melons between their legs or pass oranges to each other without using their hands. Use big melons as bowling balls to knock over pins made out of soda pop bottles. Have a taster's table where people can sample unusual fruits they've never tried before like prickly pear, loganberry, muscadine, buffaloberries, black currents, black chokeberries, dewberries, elderberries, loquats or pawpaws.

"This Ain't No Brussel Sprout" or "California Hippie Club"

Have a hippie night with lots of different kinds of salads. Set out tons of samples of sprouts for people to taste and try on their sandwich, salads or soups. Offer sprouts from legumes, such as lentils, mung, azuki, chick peas or from grassy seeds such as alfalfa, mustard, sesame, or from grains like barley, oats, and wheat. Have a contest to see who can guess where different sprouts came from.

Ice Cream Sculpting

Divide members into groups and provide each team a half gallon of vanilla ice cream, as well as a variety of edible décor such as pixie sticks for color, licorice, candy, coconut, pretzels, chocolate chips, jelly beans, sprinkles, etc. Give each team a large tray where they will create their masterpiece, as well as sculpting tools such as straws, melon ball spoons, scissors, etc. Award certificates and serve ice cream for dessert. Talk about how the Lord can sculpt us into magnificent creations if we are moldable and teachable. If you want to be able to serve the sculptures for dessert have the budding artists wear those clear, plastic gloves.

Recipes

Some of the following web sites will actually help you calculate the proper amount of ingredients to purchase according to the number of people you want to serve. They also help you find recipes based on ingredients you want to use, have great ideas for cooking for a crowd, as well as a few party ideas too:

www.allrecipes.com

www.recipes.com

www.homecooking.about.com

www.foodnetwork.com

www.bettycrocker.com

www.greatpartyrecipes.com

www.epicurious.com

www.50plusfriends.com

www.recipegoldmine.com

www.joycesfinecooking.com

www.cooks.com

Funeral Potatoes

And now for that famous Funeral Potatoes recipe that feeds a crowd so well. There are several versions floating around out there, but here is the one I use. It is extremely fattening and yummy!

Ingredients:

- 8-10 potatoes, washed, peeled, sliced OR 1 24-ounce bag frozen shredded hash brown potatoes, thawed
- 2 cans cream of chicken soup
- 2 cups sour cream
- 1 1/2 cups grated cheddar cheese
- 1/2 cup butter
- 1/2 cup onion flakes (hey, it actually uses a food storage item!)
- 1 cup crushed corn flakes, Corn Chex, or French fried onions

Preparation:

Heat oven to 350 degrees. Melt butter in a large saucepan and add soup, grated cheese, onion flakes and sour cream. Stir until mixed well. Pour over potatoes in large baking dish and mix lightly. Top with crushed corn flakes and bake, uncovered, for 35-45 minutes.

CHAPTER 16

Party Primer: Games That Mix And Mingle

"We are each of angels with only one wing and we can fly only by embracing each other."

LUCIANO DE CRESCENZO

Ice Breakers

+ **"Picture Perfect"** Have ward members either bring or make at the party a collage poster of things that describe them. The other members can try to guess who made each poster.

+ **"First Impressions"** When guests arrive tape a piece of paper onto their back and give everyone a pen or pencil. Ask the guests to write their first impressions of that person on the paper, encouraging them to write witty and kind comments. Once everyone has arrived and been given enough time to sign the others' papers, each guest can then take off the paper on his back and read what people wrote.

+ Give each person a card that has a different question and tell them they have to ask that question to everyone during the night. Write witty questions that will easily help guests to approach one another and begin fun conversations. Some examples might include "What's the difference between a duck?", "What is the worst advice you were ever given?", "What is the coolest song you've ever heard?", "What animal best describes you?", "What would you do if you won a million dollars?", "What calling would be your worst nightmare?"

+ **"Work For Your Food"** Hang a sign at the entrance that lists several groups of people and explain that they have to find the other people in a particular group and think up a cheer, short skit, song, or dance to perform before they can eat. Groups listed on the poster could include: graduated from college, worked at McDonalds, has a pet fish, knows how to snow ski, has traveled to Europe, went on a mission, served in the Nursery, etc. As groups perform they are invited to get in line for food.

+ Before the activity find out details about each member. At the activity provide each person with a list of questions he/she has to answer about the others. For every question answered correctly they earn an item for their ice cream sundae (bowl, spoon, ice cream, whip cream, bananas, etc.).

+ Create puzzles and games, using the names of ward members. Go to www.acrynym.com to create new words out of their names. Show the scrambled-up words and have them guess whose name it is. Check out www.puzzlemaker.com where you supply the words and create various word games.

+ **"Quick Change"** When people walk in to the party area give them some random play coins. Tell them they have to find enough people to make one dollar. Once they have found a group whose coins add up to a dollar they can then "buy" a place in line to get food.

+ **"The ABC's of Friendship"** As people enter the room, give them a pre-typed sheet of paper with each letter of the alphabet on it, running vertically down the page. Everyone has to find out something about the others that starts with one of the letters. For example, Tanner broke his **A**rm in 3rd grade, Brother Long plays **B**asketball, Tracey loves **C**hocolate, etc. Once their papers are filled out they can stand in line to get food, or the first ten people to complete their papers get a prize.

+ Serve different food items on each table and when a bell rings everyone can get up and change tables to sample the other foods. This will shake up their table companions as well and keep conversations fresh.

+ Play the question game. You can only talk to people in questions.

+ When everyone is gathered offer to give prizes for the first person who has a particular item in their purse, wallet or in their car such as: emergency preparedness item, picture of their family, tithing slip, band-aid, pacifier, $100 bill, the most keys, Pass Along card, gum, coin from the year 2000, breath mints, flashlight, flares, water bottle, Book of Mormon, ward directory, black pen, toy, student ID card, iPod, aspirin, mirror, etc.

+ Play games with prizes to reward those who show up for the activity on time.

+ When people enter give them a card with one specific assignment that tells them who they need to find in the room. For example, they might be told to find someone else who has broken the same bone in their body before, someone with the same college degree, someone who plays the same sport, loves the same candy bar, was born in the same state, etc. Some time during the event the people have to announce their findings.

+ Have people sit together at tables according to height, birth months, alphabetically, or some other random category.

+ Give everyone a nametag with their name misspelled. Each person, during the course of the activity, has to write down the correct spelling of everyone. The person with the most names spelled correctly wins a prize.

+ This activity will show you sides to ward members you've never seen before! Set up stations throughout the building where people can play various games that test both physical and thinking skills so that everyone will do well at something. All participants receive one bean and winners receive five. Have players rotate through stations, collecting as many beans as they can. Then, hold an auction where people bid with their beans. Auction items can be brought by each family, purchased by the committee, be donated by local venders, or be services offered by ward members.

- Hand each arrival 5 toothpicks, safety pins, beans or whatever small object complements your theme. Explain to them that they are not allowed to use the word "I" during the entire evening. Whenever they hear someone else say "I" they get to take one of their toothpicks. The person with the most toothpicks at the end of the night receives the winner's prize. You'll find that people will pay much more attention to what one another is saying!

- As guests enter the room have an announcer present them like at one of those fancy royal balls. Ask each person to think of a word that begins with the first letter of their first name that describes their hobby, talents, or likes. An example would be "Mary who likes muffins has just arrived" or "Please welcome Banker Bob." Another extension of this is to play a game where everyone stands in a circle and has to remember and repeat all of the silly names of the people before them. It's a great way to get people to remember each other's names by associating an identifying object with one another. You're sure to hear someone at church in the halls next week say something like "Hi Brother Taco Thompson."

- Before guests are allowed into the main room they have to stay at the door and greet the next person to arrive. That way there is always someone at the door and people get to feel like they're part of the success of the party.

- As guests enter have them gather in small groups in order to solve a short mystery. Clues could be given throughout your event or else the mystery game could simply be a 15 minute ice-breaker activity before the official activity begins. Winners receive a prize. Check out www.merrimysteries.com/tmm/partytips/icebreakers.htm for some great mystery scenarios.

- "It's That Time" Give everyone a piece of paper with a picture of a clock on it. Tell them to write down other people's names next to each hour. Throughout the evening have an announcer say "It's 3:00! Time for your appointment to ask them this question...!"

The guests then have to find the person they wrote down and ask each other the question that the announcer suggests.

- "Getting To Know You" Invite ward members to bring 3 items that describe themselves, their talents, or hobbies. Items could be set out on a table and people would have to guess who brought them.

- "Who's Who?" Have everyone bring their baby pictures to display on a table and place a sign next to each one with a number. Pass out a piece of paper with the numbers next to a blank line where people can write down the name of the person they think it is. Allow plenty of time for people to meander over to the table during the activity and announce the correct answers and winner at the end of the evening. The person who guesses the most pictures correctly wins a photo album or a frame.

- "Shoe Pile" Everyone takes off one of their shoes and throws it into a big pile. Then each person picks up a shoe from the pile, finds the person it belongs to, and have dessert together.

- "Sweet Success" Before the activity starts, tape pieces of candy underneath each chair. Some time during the party announce that everyone look under their chair and find their candy. Tell them to find all of the other people in the room with the same candy before they can eat it. Have each candy group sing a song, do a cheer, perform a short skit, tell jokes or think of something else they can present to the crowd.

- "Identity" When people arrive tape a card to their back that has the name of a celebrity, scripture personality, or someone else in your ward. People have to give clues to him during the evening. Once the person guesses who he is, he can take the card off his back.

- "Lucky Number 3" Tell your guests they'll be rewarded for going up to people to talk to during the activity. Give certain people some prizes to keep in their pockets. Tell them to count each person who comes up to them to talk during the evening and have them award a prize to every third person.

- "Color My World" Give each person 10 different colored pieces of candy upon arrival. They are to try to get 10 of one color by trading with other people one at a time. Those who get 10 get a prize throughout the evening.

+ **"Match-Up"** When the guests arrive give them a card with half of a couple's name written on it. During the activity they have to find their other half. Fun combinations could include: Adam and Eve, Joseph and Emma, Mickey and Minnie, Sleeping Beauty and Prince Charming, Mom and Dad, Him and Her, Salt and Pepper, Sonny and Cher, peanut butter and jelly, Acne and Adolescence, etc. Sometime during the event have the pairs go up on the stage and announce them so everyone can hear the funny combinations.

+ **"People Bingo"** or **"Human Treasure Hunt"** Make a Bingo grid with a "FREE" space in the center. In all of the other spaces, write things such as "Has been to Utah", "Has a year's supply of food storage", "Has seen the movie Napoleon Dynamite", "Born in another state", "Has pierced ears", etc. The people have to walk around the room and get the signature of a person who meets the criteria for each section. Depending on how many people are playing the game, you might want to implement a rule that a person can only sign another player's paper in two spots. The first person with a completed card wins. Some ideas for categories are: Find someone with the same color hair as you, someone who has been to Hawaii, someone who graduated from BYU, someone who is wearing a necklace, someone chewing gum, someone wearing a CTR ring.

+ **"The Thing About String"** Without telling anyone what the game is have each person cut a piece of string or yarn from a roll. Tell them to make it as long or short as they wish. Now explain that the game is to have each person take a turn and talk about themselves for as long as it takes them to wrap the string around their finger. Another variation is to assign each person a cut piece of string that has a match that was given to someone else in the room. They have to find their match, sit together and then talk until they are finished wrapping the piece around one finger.

Games That Get People To Learn About One Another

+ **"Who's Who?"** While people are waiting for dinner, have them write on a piece of paper a short fact or incident in their life that nobody knows. It can be humorous or just interesting. They should sign their name on the bottom of the paper and put it in a designated container. After dinner, the Master of Ceremonies pulls out a sheet of paper and reads the incident (except for the name). The group vocally guesses who the individual is and the real "Who's Who" must stand up or identify himself.

+ Have the group sit in chairs in a circle. Someone stands in the center of the circle and says, "Mail Call for everyone who is wearing red." Then all the people who have red on get up and switch chairs with someone else who had red on. Players cannot sit in a chair immediately beside them or in their own chair. The object is for the person in the middle to get a chair before someone else can.

+ **"Celebrity Spotlight"** Have everyone say which celebrity or famous person in history they look most like. You won't believe how entertaining this simple assignment can be!

+ **"Truth or Untruth"** Everyone thinks of 2 things about themselves that are true (I've skied on Lake Mead, I have eaten duck, etc.) and one thing that is not true but might sound reasonable (I won a burping contest, I won a baby beauty contest, etc). The group has to decide which of the three items are true and false.

+ **"M&Ms"** Get a bag of M&Ms and some small cups (like Dixie cups). As each person comes in to the room, give them a cup with a few candies and ask them not to eat any yet. After everyone has been seated in a circle, tell them you are going to go around the circle and for every color of candy they have, they have to tell the group as many things about themselves as the color represents. You can make up whatever categories you would like. For example, BLUE=Family, RED=Pets, BROWN = talents, GREEN = goals, etc.

+ **"Yes/No"** Write the word "Yes" on one side of a paper and the word "No" on the other side. Simply ask the group questions they have to answer such as "Do you have a pet?", "Can you do a cartwheel?", "Do you like spinach?" etc. Everyone will get a kick out of seeing how everyone else answers the questions.

+   **"Birthday Line"** Take some tape and make two parallel lines on the floor about a foot wide. Everyone has to stand in a row inside the lines and make sure their feet aren't touching the tape lines. They can stand side by side in the line so that the task is not impossible. Now tell them that they have to arrange each other in birthday order without stepping out of or on the lines. As people step out of the line, they're eliminated and the amount of space you have to move around increases so it gets easier.

+   Have ward members choose a partner and stand back to back with a piece of paper and pencil in hand. They then have to answer questions about the person they're standing behind (asked by the Master of Ceremonies) such as: What color are his/her eyes, hair, dress, tie, shoes, how old, etc.

+   **"Honey I Love You"** Your group should be sitting in a circle with one person in the middle. The person in the middle can go to anyone in the circle and say "Honey I love you, won't you give me a smile?" The person who was asked the question has to answer back "Honey I love you, but I just can't smile" (without smiling.) The person in the middle can do anything to the other person to make them smile except touch them.

+   **"Face To Face"** Assign half of the group to be a "1" and the other half to be a "2." Group 1 forms an inner circle and walks clockwise. Group 2 makes an outer circle walking counter-clockwise. The leader puts some music on and when he turns it off, everyone stops in front of someone in the other circle and has to do what the leader says, such as shake hands, play patty-cake, form a bridge, touch knee to knee, make funny faces at each other. You eliminate couples when they are the last ones to do what you told them to do.

+   **"Ping Pong Round Robin"** For this game you need a ping pong table, two paddles, one ball, and up to 12 people. Everyone is spread out around the table, and the two people on either end have the paddles. One person serves, drops the paddle on the table and moves in a clockwise direction around the table. The person on his left moves in and picks up the paddle to return the ball. Everyone gets a chance to hit the ball and really has to move fast! Everyone is allowed two misses and then they are out.

+ **"Give Me A Hand"** Players form a circle, cross arms, and lay their hands flat on the table or floor. Someone is picked to start the pat and each hand pats the table in its turn. If someone pats their hand twice, then the direction changes and the patting goes the other way. Remember, your arms are crossed so you have to watch carefully and wait your turn to pat. If someone lifts their hand to pat when it is not their turn, or does not pat when it is their turn, that hand is out. Play continues until there is only one hand that has not made a mistake left in the circle.

+ **"Quiz Show"** Turn any popular TV Game show into a ward version. Use questions and answers about Church history, prophets, ward trivia, scripture characters, and interesting tidbits about your own ward members. Tape record the music from TV to play so everyone really gets into the spirit of the game. Fun TV game shows that work really well are Jeopardy, Hollywood Squares, Wheel of Fortune, Who Wants to Be A Millionaire, $10,000 Pyramid.

+ **"Colored Candy"** Each person chooses a colored piece of candy when he/she enters the room. The color of the candy determines which table they will sit at. Tables should be decorated with color-coordinated tablecloths or centerpieces. Candies that work well are jelly beans, Skittles, M&Ms, lollipops, and Starbursts.

+ **"To Tell The Truth"** Invite everyone to write down a unique experience they've had, one that not many people would know. Choose 3 people to tell about the experience (one is the real person) and have people guess who is really telling the truth.

+ **"The Bean Game"** Everyone sits in a circle and is given a certain number of beans (or whatever item you want to use). Each person takes a turn telling the group something he/she has never done in their life that they think everyone else in the group has done.

Examples could include: I have never said a bad word, I have never watched the movie "E.T.", I have never been to SLC, etc. The people who have done that thing then have to throw one of their beans into the center pot. If they have not done that thing then they get to keep their beans. The winner is the person who has the most beans at the end of the game.

+ **"FROLF"** (Frisbee golf) Set up flags, construction cones or vertical markers of some kind in a park, parking lot, or inside the cultural hall. Teams have to see how many throws it takes to hit the flag on as each "hole." It's scored just like golf. Include a short lesson on how to reach our goals and aim at what's most important in life.

+ **"Bible Bowling"** Use 2 liter plastic soda bottles or plastic water bottles as bowling pins. You may want to put a little liquid in the bottom to weigh down the bottles. Line them up as bowling pins. You can use a Frisbee or any kind of sports ball to knock them down and score points. Here's where the Bible comes in (or you can use Book of Mormon verses): If someone knocks down only a few pins he/she can earn another pin by answering a scripture question that has been written down on a card and selected from a hat.

+ **"Hollywood Squares"** *or insert the name of your town instead of Hollywood* To create the look of the game show in a cultural hall, set up 3 chairs on the floor, 3 more on a very steady table behind them, and 3 more on the stage above them all. Each "celebrity" is given a giant, paper "X" and an "O". Ask questions about the scriptures, ward members, or ward history. The celebrities can give true or false answers or come up with funny answers. The players are then asked if they agree or disagree and the X or O is marked. The first team to win a Tic Tac Toe wins.

+ **"Human Foosball"** Cut some PVC pipe into different lengths to make it as much like a foosball table as possible. Put some masking tape on the floor to mark the lines where players need to stay, moving only side to side and not forward or backward. Put marks also on the PVC pipes where the players' hands need to stay in order to keep the spacing right. Use a soft kick ball or beach ball so that no one gets hurt. Include a short lesson on teamwork.

+ **"Then and Now"** Invite the older people in your ward to play a Trivia Game based on how life was then and now. Form teams of two, pairing up an older player with a younger player. It would be fun to create a slide show that compared then and now, such as pictures from American Bandstand and American Idol. Share a short history of how the Church has grown since then and where it is now.

+ **"Super Size It"** Turn any board game into a human-sized version by creating giant play money and using people as game pieces. Games that work well are Monopoly, Tic Tac Toe, Jenga (cut 2 x 4's), and Aggravation.

+ **"Three Things"** When people enter, assign them to be either a "1" or a "2." Have each "1" find a "2" to pair up with. They have to find three things they have in common and then present their findings to the rest of the group.

+ **"Tower of Babel"** People bond when they work together to complete a task. As people enter, Assign them to groups. Give each team the same materials: paper cups, empty cans, paper, balls, etc - anything you can think of. Using all the materials (points deducted for each object not used) the object is for each team to build the tallest freestanding tower without talking!

+ Play **"Pictionary"** or **"Win, Lose, or Draw"** in small groups. Some ideas for topics to be drawn are: I Love to See the Temple, Lehi's Tree of Life, The Liahona, Noah's Ark, The Last Supper, The Tower of Babel, The Rameumpton, Food Storage, Baptism, The Plan of Happiness, and the 2000 Stripling Warriors.

+ Play **"Name That Hymn"** using songs from the Primary Songbook and hymnbook.

CHAPTER 17

Mission Possible: Creating Missionary Moments

"It isn't necessary for a missionary to go outside of his country, his state, or even his own town. A true missionary need only go outside of himself."

AUTHOR UNKNOWN

Every activity you organize should be a wonderful opportunity for the ward to invite their non-member friends to. Create a friendly, non-threatening environment where members can bring their friends and neighbors to fellowship with one another. Plan your activities with non-members in mind and try to view the event through their eyes so that they will feel welcome. Plan far enough ahead so that the full-time missionaries will have enough time to pass out invitations to their investigators and warm them up to the idea. Be sure to load the missionaries up with plenty of eye-catching invitations to pass out. The more often non-members spend time in your church building and around members, the more comfortable they will feel when approached by the missionaries. Here are some ideas to help your members get the courage to invite their friends, as well as activities that work especially well for introducing non-members to the Church.

- Let members know ahead of time that if they bring a non-member guest to an activity both they and their guest will receive a special treat. The treat could be as simple as a plate of cookies, a coupon for a free ice cream cone (donated by a local vender), an inexpensive item from a dollar store, a bag of candy or even a bag of "starter" for Amish Friendship Cake attached to a wooden spoon.

- **"Sweet Friendships"** Encourage members to invite their friends to a dessert social where they will be treated to musical numbers and lots of decadent treats. Set up tables around the room for each auxiliary to decorate in a way that explains their function and activities. Invite the presidencies to stand at their tables to answer questions and talk to guests. Include table displays on the Family History Center, food storage, the Boy Scouts, and the Proclamation on the Family. Focus on the sweet friendships that are made in the Church and how the gospel is sweet!

- **"A Week In The Life of a Mormon"** Plan a week full of events that highlight some of the things Latter-day Saints do to live the gospel. Members can invite their friends to as many activities as they want for a full missionary blitz. Showcasing a week is also a different way to display information at an Open House event. For example:

  Monday – Family Home Evening
  Tuesday – Enrichment Night or Missionary Splits
  Wednesday – Youth Activity Night (Mutual)
  Thursday – Boy Scouts and Cub Scouts
  Friday – Achievement Day or Family History Night
  Saturday – Ward Party
  Sunday – Service and worship

- **"FAQ Attack"** Invite non-members to meet the bishop or Mission President to ask any question they want. Encourage the priesthood leader to share a short message before the question and answer session and end with some yummy refreshments.

- **"Around the World"** Create an international flair by setting up booths that represent countries where members have served missions. Encourage returned missionaries to share their experiences of living in that country and provide a tasty sample of some of the food from each country.

• **"Cleanliness Is Next to Godliness"** Hold a car wash but don't charge money. Offer to wash cars for free as a community service and give drivers Pass-Along cards.

• **"Family Home Evening 101"** or **"FHE for Dummies"** Encourage members to invite their friends to learn about Family Home Evening. Organize the event like an actual Family Home Evening with songs, short lessons, games, activities and, of course, refreshments. Set up booths around the room with displays on how to create Family Home Evening packets, make visual aids for lessons, ideas for games and activities, and samples of favorite snacks. You could also hold a round-robin schedule where guests rotate through short classes that teach them how to incorporate service into their Family Home Evenings, ideas for young children, involving teens in lessons, how to make a flannel board for visual aids, tips for Empty Nesters, etc.

• **"Bigger/Better Scavenger Hunt"** Divide the guests into smaller groups who are given a random object. They have to go into the nearby neighborhood and exchange it for a bigger, better item. Encourage groups to share Pass Along cards with people they meet in the street. Share refreshments at the end of the evening and present awards for the group who came back with the most creative, biggest item.

• **"The Great American Race"** Divide guests into groups or families and have them go out into the community to gather clues and items you have left for them ahead of time. You could also let them be creative and just give them a theme, such as chopsticks and they have to go to a location that has something to do with chopsticks and bring back an item to prove they were there. Load each group up with Pass Along cards and give a prize to the group who was able to pass out the most cards during their race.

• **"Mission Possible"** This activity could be to help families know how to prepare their sons and daughters to serve full-time missions and create a "Missionary Training Center" atmosphere in their homes. It could also be a motivating event to inspire older couples to want to serve full-time missions. Invite returned missionaries to talk about what to expect and include all expects of preparation from sewing on a button to cooking a meal to exercising and staying spiritual fit. Encourage the full-time missionaries to share their experiences and play fun games like "Pin the name tag on the missionary", tricycle races, "Throw the ring around the backpack."

• **"A Boy Scout Is"** Host a merit badge clinic for boys working on advancement toward their Eagle Scout award. Members could choose an area they could confidently teach by looking at the choices at www.meritbadge.com Teachers need to be officially registered as merit badge counselors in order for the boys to receive credit. Invite Boy Scouts from other Troops in your area so they will have an opportunity to spend some time in your church building and get to know the members. Work with your Scoutmaster to make this a big, successful event.

• **"Box of Love"** Every month or quarter set out an empty box for each missionary, college student or military member who is serving far from home. Encourage the ward to bring items that can be sent, including non-perishable snacks, letters, cartoons, drawings, toiletries, etc. Tape record greetings from the people in the ward on to a cassette tape or film them on a DVD.

• **"Military moms"** If you live near a military base you probably know how difficult it is for the wives of deployed servicemen to keep things running at home. Have your ward make Easter baskets for the children of soldiers or create special Mother's Day baskets for the women whose husbands won't be there to pamper them on that special day. You can get ideas for other ways you could help by talking to the Chaplain on base or the organization in charge of military wives. Let the military families know you appreciate their sacrifices and that they are always welcome in your ward.

- **"Blanket Brigade"** Make or gather blankets and coats that could be delivered to the homeless shelters during cold, winter months. Attach a note of love and hope to them along with the name of the Church.

- **"A+"** or **"The Gift Of Life"** Invite your local blood bank or call the American Red Cross to host a blood drive at your church building. Members could be volunteers and donors during the event. Call 1-800-GIVE-LIFE to find out what you would need to do to set up a drive in your community.

- **"Stake Missionary Spotlight"** Invite the ward and stake missionaries to shine by hosting an Open House for non-members. Put together care packages for the missionaries who are serving from your ward.

- **"The Voice of America"** Offer to register voters in your area for upcoming elections. Find out how your ward can help at the booths. Normally there is a training class that volunteers must attend. Let the community see that your ward is interested in making your town a better place. Let them see through your active example what the 12th Article of Faith is all about.

- **"Adopt A Mile"** Talk to your local city government about their "Adopt A Mile" program and how your ward could get involved. You will need to commit to cleaning up a certain stretch of a road or waterway for an extended length of time. Be sure to get approval from your bishop. You could rotate the monthly assignment through the various ward auxiliaries to help with this ongoing service project. The ward will then be given a sign to post with its name on it and the Church's community involvement will be reflected in how well you keep the area clean!

- Take a picture of everyone at each of your ward activities and send copies to the full-time missionaries who are serving from your ward. It will be fun for them to see the growing children and let them know you're thinking of them. It's impossible for missionaries to get too much mail or loving support.

- **"Time warp"** Encourage everyone to dress in time period costumes. You could choose a particular era to focus on or cover the history of the world. Talk about how the gospel was presented on the earth during those times. Sample food, music and games from each dispensation.

- **"The Worth Of A SOLE"** Assign a different kind of shoe to represent each kind of church member. There are some cute Relief Society skits on-line that could easily be adapted to fit the ward. Cut footprints out of paper, making paths all over the floor. Have someone sing "I walked Today Where Jesus Walked." Decorate with different kinds of shoes and have a speaker talk about the worth of a sole (soul). Set up little signs on display tables or make big posters with sayings like:
  - "Don't let your missionary work sneak up on you!" (*sneakers*)
  - "Being a Mormon is uplifting" (*high heels*)
  - "Buckle down and keep the commandments" (*shoes with buckles*)
  - "Don't get tied up with unimportant things" (*shoelaces*)
  - "Don't be a loafer – live the gospel!" (*loafers*)
  - "Just open your mouth to share the gospel and converse!" (*Converse shoes*)
  - "Never let your standards slip" (*slippers*)
  - "Don't flip flop your values." (*flip flops*)
  - "Get a kick out of the gospel!" (*cleats*)
  - "Keep on your toes with your temple service" (*ballet slippers*)
  - "Never let your testimony go flat" (*flats*)

  You get the idea …
- **"Black Name Tag"** Adopt a missionary serving in your area. Call the mission home to find out if there are any missionaries who aren't receiving emotional support from their families and offer to send them letters of encouragement or care packages of love. If you want to learn about the LDS statistics in your area go to www.mormonhaven.com/geninfo.htm and scroll down to the LDS Almanac area.

◆ **"Missionary Messages"** A table could be set out each month with stationery, note cards, stickers, markers, pens and pencils so that the members can write letters of encouragement to the missionaries who are serving from the ward. All of the letters could then be mailed together in a special care package from the ward. Similar packages of cards and letters could be mailed to any ward members serving in the military away from home or college students away for the school year.

CHAPTER 18

Family Matters: Keeping The Kids Happy & Safe

"Kids: they dance before they learn
there is anything that isn't music."

———————————

WILLIAM STAFFORD

Children can create a wonderful feeling of excitement and joy at a ward activity, but they can also destroy the ambiance if not monitored carefully. Sometimes parents are the only ones who think their little darling is adorable while he shreds the paper tablecloth. Learn to perfect the art of gently reminding parents to control their children. Parents can take offense easily, so remind them in a loving way and offer plenty of activities to keep little hands and minds busy. Children can naturally turn to destruction when bored. Enlist the help of your Primary presidency. Make a friendly announcement at the beginning of each activity about children showing respect, parents caring for the little ones' safety, and showing reverence for the building, especially the chapel. Below are some ideas to help you create a ward activity that is enjoyable for the children. When the children are happy, their parents are happy and will want to return to your next event!

+ If you have a wide gap between "newlyweds" and "nearly deads" in your ward, you might want to plan a two-tiered activity where older people can have some quiet visiting time together before families with young children join the party.

+ Set up some tents and tunnels for the children to play in. Assign someone to monitor the area for safety.

+ Designate a separate room or area off to the side of the main event where supervised children can color pictures, work on crafts, watch a movie, and play with toys.

+ Recruit help from the Young Women and Scouts in your ward who need service hours to earn their awards. You could ask them to baby-sit the younger children in shifts of 20-30 minutes. Well-behaved children can stay with their parents.

+ Make shrinky dinks as necklaces or ornaments. See www. shrinkydinks.com for instructions. (Isn't it amazing that there is a web site for everything?)

+ Set out rolls of different colored poster paper and let the children draw like crazy with crayons, chalk, or washable markers. You can give them an assignment such as to draw a picture for the Primary room or for the missionaries' apartment or else you can just let their creativity wander. You'll need to have a helper monitor them closely who can remind them that the only drawing to be done is on the actual paper.

+ Whatever your party's theme is, you can easily come up with some version of "Pin the Tail on the Donkey."

+ Find an artist in your ward who could draw a picture of some kind of scenery that goes with your theme on a roll of poster paper. Have the little children add items to it such as sea creatures on ocean scenery or pirates added onto a ship design, etc.

+ Another game that is always a hit with kids is a good old-fashioned bean bag throw. Cut out a box with some holes and then paint or decorate it to coordinate with your party theme.

+ Throw a tarp on the floor in a corner and set out some big containers with hidden treasures buried in rice, beans or sand.

+ Invite the children to create edible jewelry by stringing cereal or candy into necklaces or bracelets.

- Set out items on a table where children can decorate bookmarks, cookies, cards, or scrapbook pages.

- Fill a jar with small items that go along with your theme (candy, toys, decorative items, etc.) and have the children guess how many are inside. Okay, parents can play too. Leave some paper and pencils on a table during the event and announce the big winner before the closing prayer.

- Find a young woman in the ward (or any willing and capable person!) who can do face painting for the children during the event.

- If your event is outside, supply plenty of sidewalk chalk so the children can create masterpieces while the adults talk.

- Provide a clay or play dough table. Have a contest to see who can make items that correlate with your activity's theme.

- Set up a table with various food items and have the children create faces out of them on a plate. You could have a contest to see which creation looks the most like the bishop, the missionaries in your ward, Book of Mormon characters, or whatever.

- Provide a table where children can put together their very own Family Home Evening lesson packet. Using those large, brown paper bags from the grocery store, cut the top part down so it's the size of a manila folder, complete with tab. The children can then fill the bag with pictures they color to go with a story you provide about a particular gospel principle. Provide supplies so they can create a refrigerator magnet with a scripture, game pieces for a family activity, and recipe cards for their snack at the end of their Family Home Evening lesson.

- Help the children make cute puppets that could be used during Family Home Evening lessons. Show different kinds of puppets and supply a puppet theater where the children can create their own shows and possibly perform something for the ward by the end of the night. Invite the kids to bring their own puppets from home.

- Buy a few of those small, plastic balloon pumps and set out long balloons so the children can design their own crazy hats and balloon animals. Be sure to have an adult monitor the table so that little ones don't choke on the balloons. Ask the Young Men, Young Women, Scouts, or Activity Day leaders to provide a lesson on how to make balloon animals and do face painting. After the youth learn how to do it they'll be a terrific resource for you to call upon during upcoming activities!

+ Piñatas can be found to go with any theme these days, so include one at your next activity! Fill it with candy that is wrapped, rather than loose candy, and include a few inexpensive toys. Start with the smallest child and work your way up. Every child gets three swings only; otherwise you'll be working on the piñata for hours. Children can choose to be blindfolded or not. The most important thing is to make sure that all of the children stand very far away from the person swinging the bat. Their excitement will cause them to keep sneaking up closer, so you'll have to keep reminding them. Before you do the piñata, hang it up somewhere as one of the decorations and invite the children to decorate bags they can use to fill with candy once the piñata breaks.

+ Form a "Babysitters' Club" that helpers are inducted into after each activity. Hold a special Babysitters' Club party every now and then to thank them for their help during activities.

+ Set out tables where children can be kept busy with crossword puzzles, word scrambles, riddles, anagrams, etc. Award prizes for children who complete the challenges.

+ Create a station somewhere in the room where the children can work on and pass off one of their "Faith In God" requirements. Ask the Primary presidency to help you identify which ones might correlate well with the theme of your activity. The kids will then leave the party feeling like they have really accomplished something and the Primary leaders will be grateful you included them in such a meaningful way.

Activity Resources For Kids

www.funology.com/boredombusters/index.htm
www.kinderart.com
www.apples4theteacher.com
www.education-world.com
www.kidsdomain.com
www.makingfriends.com
www.enchantedlearning.com
www.orientaltrading.com
www.cdkenterprises.com/coloring/index.shtml#holidays
www.kiddyhouse.com
www.activityvillage.co.uk
www.simplifun.com

CHAPTER 19

Publicity 101

"All publicity is good, except an
obituary notice."

BRENDAN F. BEHAN

Publicity is KEY to having a successful activity. If no one knows about the event then no matter how much time and money you've spent organizing the affair, you'll only have your relatives show up. You need to start advertising weeks in advance and use every means possible to remind people. Members of the Church are incredibly busy, so if you let them know far in advance then you have a better chance that they'll hold the date of your activity open. Even still, you'll have to remind them several times.

The trick to designing posters and flyers is to create them so they advertise just enough information to whet the members' appetite and to convince them that through their attendance at the event they will be blessed.

Whenever you involve a lot of people in the activity program you'll automatically have more attendance. Consider inviting the ward choir, Primary children, the Young Men or Young Women, Relief Society sisters or any other combination of people to sing, dance or perform at each ward activity. That way you'll at least have those people and their families attend! President James E. Faust wisely stated, "We should bear in mind that the success of a given activity cannot always be judged by its size. Rather, it must be judged by its effect on the lives of those participating." ("Strengthening the Inner Self," *Ensign*, Feb. 2003, 4.)

One of your best advertising techniques is word of mouth. If people had fun at your last activity, then they'll plan on attending your next one, as well as tell their friends about it. Get people to talk it up.

At least one month before an activity, advertise in the following locations:

+ Your ward bulletin every Sunday
+ On your ward bulletin board in the hall
+ Posters in each foyer on an easel, table, or wall
+ Posters in the Relief Society room, Primary room, Young Women's room, Scout room, Nursery
+ Poster on or near the bishop's door (with permission)
+ Flyers on cars in the parking lot
+ Send emails
+ Get Home Teachers and Visiting Teachers to spread the word or pass out invitations to the people they visit
+ Create a Yahoo or Google Group for your ward and post weekly messages about upcoming events
+ Snail mail flyers or postcards
+ Use your sign-up sheets as a form of advertisement by making them eye-catching and informative. Be sure to keep your requests for help light and guilt-free. For example, in December you could write on Christmas paper "Making a list, checking it twice; if you could help it sure would be nice!"
+ Make announcements in person during Sunday School and all of the auxiliary meetings. Better yet, do a funny skit or wear a costume to catch their attention rather than simply tell ward members about the event. Get creative!
+ Recruit the help of the youth or Primary children to dress up according to the theme of the event and pass out flyers.
+ Plan several months ahead so you'll be able to include information about your events in your ward newsletter or ward calendar.

- During your activity, start talking up your next activity.
- Give the Bishopric member who is conducting in Sacrament meeting an announcement to read over the pulpit.
- Attach an inexpensive, catchy item to a flyer so they won't just throw away the announcement as soon as you walk away.
- Make announcement cards with magnetic strips on the back so members can post them on their refrigerators to remind them daily of the upcoming activity.
- Check out www.partyinvitations.com for clever ideas on making your invitations and flyers more interesting and eye popping.
- Try using a free invitation company like www.evite.com so people can RSVP online and you can get a better head count before the event to help you know how much food to buy.
- Enclose a flyer with the Sunday bulletin that is passed out before Sacrament meeting.
- Design a web site where people can go to get all of the information and maybe even win a prize for visiting the site.
- Create a wallpaper design you can email to people to put on their computers to remind them of the upcoming event.
- Advertise in person at the next Enrichment Night activity, Cub Scout Pack meeting, Mutual Night or other event in the ward.
- Give ward members an item they have to take home and bring back on the date of the party. Some examples are:
    - Give them empty baby food jars they have to return filled with candy that will be used as place setting décor.
    - Take home an empty brown bag and return it decorated to be filled with popcorn at a movie night.
    - Decorate a plastic cup that will be used as their drinking cup all night at the party.
    - Decorate a paper bag or tin can that could be used as a luminaria outside the entrance of the party.
    - A Styrofoam ball they have to turn into an ornament.
    - A bag or box they have to put items in to swap with someone else or put a "White Elephant" gift in to play the game.

- A paper puzzle for them to figure out at home which gives them a clue about getting a prize or winning a game at the upcoming activity.

- Set out a table display with props and decorative items that ward members will see at the next activity. Include paper and pencils so people can sign up to bring food items or RSVP early to win a prize.

- Wear one of those sandwich boards with information about the activity outside in parking lot or in the building (not in chapel). If you're too shy for such outrageous behavior then bribe some of the youth to do it for a payment of candy bars. They'll do almost anything for food.

- Print out T-shirts or buttons that say, "Ask me about our next ward party" and have your committee or some youth wear them during weekly activities.

- Have your committee personally call families to remind them of the event a few days before the party.

- Recruit someone on your committee or an enthusiastic youth to stand outside the parking lot waving a big sign that advertises the event. Teach them how to do flips with the sign and move it around a lot to catch people's attention as they drive in and out of the Church grounds.

Websites to help you design invitations and flyers:

www.free-invitations-online.com

www.perfect-printable-invitations.com

www.print-free-cards.com

www.polkadotdesign.com

www.avery.com/homecorner/creations_occasions_03.html

www.internetfamilyfun.com/printables.htm

www.parentingteens.about.com/od/cardmaking/ss/
birthdayparty.htm

www.activityvillage.co.uk

www.kidsturncentral.com/birthdays/bdinvites.htm

www.familycrafts.about.com/od/birthdaypartyinvitations/a/
printbirthinv.htm

www.magicbob2000.com/invitations.html

www.greetingcardinsanity.com

www.canonprintplanet.com/party_kidbday.shtml

www.hallmark.com

www.myfuncards.com

www.123greetings.com

www.bluemountain.com

Also, see the list of Clip Art websites in Chapter 21.

CHAPTER 20

Decorations: The Silver Lining

"The ornament of a house is the friends
who frequent it."

RALPH WALDO EMERSON

Your decorations can really set the tone and mood for a ward activity. They don't have to be elaborate or expensive, but if attention to detail is given then the guests will feel that and will appreciate the time and preparation. Here are a few tips to help you set up a party that screams, "I'm so glad you came! You're going to have a ball!" Check out party-supply stores and web sites to get ideas for centerpieces and décor items. Often times you can duplicate the idea much less expensively. To cut costs, share decorations with other wards or stakes. Make a few phone calls and you're sure to make some new friends as well. Find out what others are doing and suggest sharing a decoration closet. There is no need to reinvent the wheel if someone else has already put in a lot of effort and is willing to share.

Entrance

+ Don't neglect decorations on the outside of the building. A few well-placed signs, balloons, or decorative items let the arriving guests know they're really in for a special occasion. It's fun to set out a large sign or poster and have the guests sign it or add their own artwork to it as they're entering the party.

+ Create a special gateway that people will walk through so they will truly leave the outside world and cares behind. If you're having a western hoe-down, make those western swinging saloon doors by taping painted cardboard half-doors to the hinges. If your party has an Arabian or circus theme you could hang inexpensive sheets to give the ambiance of entering a tent. Hang beads, streamers, garlands or vines from doorways at the entrance, restroom, or other areas of the building to keep people in the thematic mood.

+ Using cardboard, create cut-outs of characters, creatures, or people to welcome guests as they arrive. Ask a store that sells appliances if you can have their boxes and they'll be more than happy to give them to you. Paint a base-coat to cover dark print or use long rolls of butcher paper to give you a clean background to design on. If you're not artistic, find someone in your ward who is to help you or ask the Young Men and Young Women to add the project into their weekly Mutual activity. You'll be amazed at how creative they can be. Whenever you involve lots of people in party preparations, the more invested they will be in attending and helping it to be a success.

+ It's so easy nowadays to create banners on your home computer, so create a welcome banner that introduces guests to the theme and directs them to where they need to go. Make posters, banners and small flyers that can be placed all over the building, in the parking lot, in bathroom stalls, on the lawn, and on chairs. People really respond well to humor, so keep your designs light-hearted, informative, and positive.

+ Set up a stand or table at the entrance with a guest book for people to sign to let them know their attendance is appreciated. You could also choose door prize winners from the list. Have them sign a book or simply write their name on a slip of paper that is then placed inside a thematic item such as a pumpkin, hat, basket or decorative container.

+ Provide nametags and markers at the entry door to encourage guests to learn one another's names. Be sure to also provide a small waste basket, so after the guests peel off the sticky backing they'll know what to do with the paper.

+ A lot of people like to hang seasonal flags outside of their homes, so perhaps you could borrow one or two to hang outside the party entrance.

+ Assign someone to be the party greeter at the door. The greeter should be in costume and speak with an accent if your theme requires one. The Young Men and Young Women could be an eager welcoming committee if you encourage them to be creative. Have your greeter hand out items such as leis, nametags, hats, bandanas, headbands, glow sticks and such to get people in the mood and prepare them to be active participants in the activity rather than passive observers.

+ Decorate the lawn with those tacky pink flamingos or beach umbrellas or something that tells arriving guests to expect something extra special.

+ Lighted candles are not allowed inside Church buildings because of fire hazard liability, however they are allowed outside. Put sand in colored lunch bags and light tea candles to create inexpensive luminarias along the pathway to the party entrance. Have a bucket of water nearby to pour on the bags if they do happen to catch on fire. Assign someone to check on them throughout the evening. You could also recruit the help of Scouts to create tin can luminarias by poking holes in tin cans with a hammer and nail. They can create designs that complement your party theme.

Main Area

+ Tie a few balloons outside the party location to help guests find the party entrance. Always use an odd number of balloons in a bouquet and space them out so they're slightly different heights. Place balloon bouquets at the entrance, on tables, near doors, on the stage, or in clusters around the floor. You can create decorative weights to hold helium balloons down by simply wrapping a brick in pretty paper that coordinates with your theme. You could also attach the balloon to a weighted item that goes with your theme, such as a large stuffed animal or toy, shoes, sports equipment, potted plants, soda cans. At the end of the evening, send the children home with a balloon as their take-home gift. Put slips of paper that have prizes written on them inside some of the balloons. At the end of the activity, tell the guests to go pop a balloon and collect their prize at a certain location. Many local stores and fast food restaurants will donate prizes if you just ask them. Don't be shy; the worst thing the store manager can say is no!

+ Try to create a focus point in the main party space that boldly announces the theme and where a Master of Ceremonies can speak and be seen from any point in the room.

+ Set up a digital camera station where you can print out pictures of the party guests for them to take home and remember their fun evening.

+ Encourage members to dress up in costume, according to your theme. That's the cheapest decoration there is! Party supply stores might even allow you to wear a costume for free if you tell people about their store. You can also supply inexpensive accessories to help dress people up to match your room decor, such as giving them a lei, a cowboy bandana, a pirate patch, Marti Gras beads, 60's necklace, glow-in-the-dark bracelets, construction hats, etc.

+ Using cardboard you get from large appliance boxes, design one of those photo stand-ins where people can put their heads in and have a funny body.

+ Lighting can set the mood extremely well, so invest in some good uplights and Christmas tree strands. Use uplights under silk plants or around displays. Hang Christmas tree lights from the ceiling, wrapped around silk plants, running along walls, or carefully taped to the floor as directional paths.

+ Create sitting areas and cozy vignettes around the room where people can gather, take pictures, and visit more intimately. Arrange a few couches, cushy chairs, bean bags, or hammock in a corner with a themed backdrop.

- Work with an experienced sound system person to create background music that isn't overbearing but that sets the mood. Assign someone to care for the equipment and adjust the sound during prayers, speeches, and other entertainment. Talk to the Stake Young Women and Young Men leaders to get a good list of appropriate songs that are Church-approved. They're used to planning youth dances and can also be a great resource for decorations, games, and ideas to keep the teenagers interested and involved in your activity.

- There's nothing wrong with posting an announcement in the ward Sunday bulletin to request certain décor items that people might have and be willing to let you borrow for your event. You'll be amazed what people have lurking in their basements and garages.

- Dangle things from ceilings such as streamers, lights, ribbons, paper cutouts, toys, or any lightweight object that goes with your theme.

- You probably spray some nicely scented potpourri right before guests arrive in your home, right? Try spraying some in the party area before your event and people will be pleasantly surprised. You can transform a regular Cultural Hall into a tropical paradise or a cozy cottage or an Asian garden just by spraying the right scent around the space.

- Stores often have elaborate seasonal displays made out of cardboard that they would be willing to give you if you simply ask the manager. Keep your eyes open and plan ahead.

- Turn any old container into a pretty holder for flowers, bread, candy, nuts, chips or party favors by wrapping it in fabric, taffeta, or cellophane. Tie it all together with ribbons or raffia.

Tables

- There is nothing more boring than a flat table with food set on it. YAWN! Take a hint from the professional banquet displays and create lifts and levels to add eye appeal. Before you put the table cloth on set down bowls, upside-down pots, paint cans, boxes, and other strong bases that create varying heights. You may need several tablecloths in order to drape fabric around all of the shapes. Use a different colored fabric below the table's centerpiece for an added splash on the focal point. Now place the food dishes and décor items on the table. So much more festive!

+ Although confetti is festive and comes in many shapes and sizes nowadays, remember that you'll have to clean up every little piece and that small children will be tempted to put it in their mouths. You may want to reconsider.

+ For something different, buy about 2 1/2 yards of clearance fabric to cover the long tables. You'll find some very festive fabric and can pick some up very inexpensively after each holiday so you'll be ready for next year's party!

+ Invite ward members to be in charge of supplying decorations for one of the tables. Give them the theme and let them run wild with it. You could even offer a prize for the best table.

+ To cut costs on paper goods, ask families to bring their own plates and utensils. Once people get over the initial shock, they'll get used to the change and you can spend the money you saved on other aspects of the event. This works especially well for potlucks. Of course, inevitably there will be those who forget to bring their plates and utensils, so you will need to keep a small supply on hand.

+ The most important thing to remember about creating a table centerpiece is that it shouldn't stand so tall that people can't see each other from opposite sides of the table while sitting down and trying to converse! Next time you're at church, sit down on a chair at one of the tables and measure the maximum height that would be appropriate for an average adult. A good rule of thumb is to keep the height 12 inches or less. A small child's vision may be obstructed a bit, but they won't be nearly as interested in conversation as the adults will be! A centerpiece on a food table or on a stage can be much larger.

+ Provide markers near the cups so guests can write their names on their drinks and, hopefully, only use one during the evening rather than several.

* Make bundles of one napkin and utensils wrapped together with raffia or a ribbon and put them in a large basket for people to grab and go or at each place setting to ensure everyone has what they need.

* You can dress up a food table by designing your own specialty toothpicks. Print small pictures of an item that goes with your theme, cut them out and tape them to each toothpick. Place the toothpicks in fruit or veggie platters.

* A table centerpiece doesn't have to be just for decoration, it can be functional too! Create a centerpiece arrangement out of lollipops, cookies, candy, cupcakes, breadsticks or some other part of the meal. Use a dish and arrange pieces as if you were designing a floral centerpiece.

* Learn how to fold napkins in creative ways to dress up place settings, even with paper napkins. Go to www.napkinfoldingguide. com for lots of ideas. For a pretty layered look, put two different-colored napkins together and flair out.

* Use food items to create whimsical table centerpieces. For example, if you're having a western theme, stand three zucchini plants upright in a pot and attach a mum to one of them with a toothpick to make it look like a blooming cactus plant.

* For a festive, but simple decoration, stuff colored tissue paper in bags, boxes, boots, or containers that complement your theme.

CHAPTER 21

Website Resources

"Getting information off the Internet is like taking a drink from a fire hydrant."

MITCHELL KAPOR

WEBSITES

Ideas

www.theideadoor.com/wardactivities.html
www.reasontoparty.com
www.family.com
www.familyfun.com
www.homemakingcottage.com
www.lightplanet.com/mormons/actcomm.htm
www.promoms.org/latter-day-living/activity-ideas/
www.ywconnection.com
www.dialmproductions.com
www.partysuppliesshop.com/party-planning/
www.holiday-party-decorations.com
www.diynetwork.com
www.dotcomwomen.com/food/entertaining/index.shtml

Decorations & supplies

www.orientaltrading.com
www.4funparties.com

www.shindigz.com
www.lillianvernon.com
www.kidspartyfun.com
www.partycity.com
www.celebrateexpress.com
www.partypro.com
www.partysecret.com
www.partysupplieshut.com
www.bulkpartysupplies.com
www.partysuppliesworld.com
www.partypop.com
www.iparty.com
www.partyworlddirect.com

Special Equipment

www.buycostumes.com
www.prettypartyplace.com
www.everythingelementary.com
www.fun4allpartys.com
www.rentalhq.com
www.stumpsparty.com
www.celebrationfantastic.com
www.lolliesgalore.com
www.classicpartyrentals.com
www.gourmetsnow.com
www.giddyupponies.com

Skits and Plays

www.scoutorama.com/skit/
www.thesource4ym.com/skits
www.macscouter.com/skits/
www.geocities.com/pocolocoplayers/short.html
www.christiancrafters.com/skits.html
www.usscouts.org/usscouts/skits.asp
www.djmorton.demon.co.uk/scouting/campfire.htm
www.42explore.com/skits&plays.htm

www.burtleburtle.net/bob/scout/index.html
www.drama.eserver.org/plays/
www.lazybeescripts.co.uk/Sketches/Index.htm
www.playsandmusicals.co.uk/frame.htm

Clip Art

www.christysclipart.com
www.debanae.net/clipart.html
www.jennysmith.net
www.lds-images.com
www.lds.mycityport.com/clipart.htm
www.awesomeclipartforeducators.com/
www.oneil.com.au/lds/pictures.html
www.lds.org/hf/art
www.ldsecards.com
www.faithclipart.com
www.inspiregraphics.com/lds/main.html
www.clipartlibrary.us/

Index

P

Patriotic 14, 23, 42, 79–80,
     95–96, 100–101, 140, 146
Peanuts 36, 49, 94, 110, 126
Photography 13
Pioneers 105
Polar bears 15
Popcorn 25
Presidents 38, 42
Prophets 14, 197
Puzzles 11, 29, 100, 190, 212

S

Safety 4, 8, 36, 62, 73, 90, 192,
     209–210
Science 17, 23, 37, 55, 69, 107,
     113
Scriptures 55
Service 7, 14, 20, 23, 25, 36,
     60–63, 66–67, 71, 80, 90,
     93, 103, 114, 118, 123, 134,
     138, 144, 153, 155–156,
     160–162, 170, 203,
     205–206, 210
Sesame Street 53
Spain 51, 236
Sports 34–35, 57, 78, 89, 99, 112,
     127, 145, 198, 224, 237
Spring 10, 34, 54, 64, 137

T

Temples 14, 28, 93, 139, 157, 180
Transportation 79

V

Valentine 38–40

W

Weather 17, 34, 45, 55
Winnie The Pooh 103
Winter 148
World 22, 55, 68, 70, 79, 132,
     139, 140, 167, 193, 202

About the Author

Trina Bates Boice grew up in sunny California and later braved the cold and snow at Brigham Young University where she earned two Bachelor's degrees. While there she competed on the BYU Speech & Debate team, and BYU Ballroom Dance Team. She was President of the National Honor Society Phi Eta Sigma and ASBYU Secretary of Student Community Services.

Trina also studied at the University of Salamanca in Spain and later returned to serve a full-time mission to Madrid, Spain for the Church of Jesus Christ of Latter-day Saints. She earned a Master's degree from California College for Health Sciences. She worked as a Legislative Assistant for a Congressman in Washington D.C. and wrote a column called "The Boice Box" for a local newspaper in Georgia where she lived for 15 years. She has a real estate license, travel agent license, a Black Belt in Tae Kwon Do, and helps her husband, Tom, with their real estate appraisal and investment companies. If she told you what she really did all day, she would have to kill you.

Trina was honored in November 2004 as George Bush's "Points of Light Volunteer" and also received the President's Lifetime

Volunteer Service award. She was the "2004 Honor Young Mother of the Year" for the state of California and lives in beautiful Carlsbad with her four wonderful sons. They keep busy with Scouting, all kinds of sports, and are surfer wannabes now that they live closer to the beach. They now brave the cold and snow of Utah together to go skiing and visit family!

Trina currently teaches Seminary and works in the beautiful San Diego Temple. Check out her website at www.boicebox.com.

Trina she selected her niece, Brittany, to do the illustrations at the start of each chapter for this book!

About the Illustrator

Brittany Long is the daughter of Trina's twin. She entered the world during the October 1990 General Conference as the Mormon Tabernacle Choir sang "Hallelujah!"

A born book and art enthusiast, she has marched through her teenage years with a book under each arm and a pencil behind her ear. In addition to getting straight A's and being top of the class, Brittany participates in her high school's theatre department as an actress and director and enjoys it very much. She has played the piano for more than a decade, and in any spare time she finds loves drawing as well as reading, writing, acting, speaking French, cooking Pasta Roni, being vegetarian, and procrastinating.

Brittany's ambition is to become an author and one day illustrate her own books. Until then, she writes for her English teacher and posts her doodles on her personal website at www.brytning. hatesmonday.com. She lives in Las Vegas, Nevada with her family and her beagle, Joy.